THE Prenatal EXERCISE HANDBOOK

THE *Prenatal* EXERCISE HANDBOOK

Fitness and Health in Pregnancy

Jenny Whitby

SIDGWICK & JACKSON
LONDON

First published in Great Britain in 1989 by
Sidgwick & Jackson Limited

Copyright © 1989 Jenny Whitby

Illustrations by Nicky Dupays
Design by Paul Watkins

The author and publisher are grateful to
Professor Beard of St Mary's Hospital,
London, for kind permission to
reproduce his article on Amniocentesis

ISBN 0 283 99663 3

Photoset by
Rowland Phototypesetting Limited
Bury St Edmunds, Suffolk
Printed in Hong Kong
for Sidgwick & Jackson Limited
1 Tavistock Chambers, Bloomsbury Way
London WC1A 2SG

Contents

Foreword

I met Jenny Whitby during the years I was giving antenatal classes and was immediately impressed by her understanding of pregnant women, both physically and emotionally. Particularly, I appreciated her common sense approach to the whole subject. She shares my belief in balance and moderation in everything pertaining to pregnancy and labour.

In this book she covers all aspects of pregnancy including the changes and problems which can occur. She explains clearly and simply a programme of physical exercises and breathing techniques which can be of great benefit, before, during, and after labour.

I can recommend *The Prenatal Exercise Handbook* to any pregnant woman and feel sure that it will help everyone who reads it and follows the advice contained in it.

Betty Parsons MBE
London 1988

Acknowledgments

I would very much like to express my thanks to all of the following:

Professor Beard, for his help and sensitivity; Dr Catherine O'Connor, for answering my endless queries; Betty Parsons for her invaluable teaching; all the girls who have attended my prenatal classes and from whom I have learned so much; and everyone who has helped me retain my sanity while working with a word processor!

Introduction

When I first carried out research on the material available to help keep mums-to-be fit and healthy, I was amazed at how few comprehensive guides there were. The absolute fundamentals seemed, somehow, to be glossed over, leaving many simple questions unanswered. I was all the more aware of this because, in the course of teaching exercise classes for over ten years, I have constantly been asked the same, surprisingly basic questions.

So much information and 'advice' is thrown in the direction of expectant mothers but how are you to differentiate between the facts and the old wives' tales? How do you know which exercises to perform, what foods are good or bad, and what clothes to wear? And where do you go should anything go wrong?

What I have written is a basic handbook, drawing on my teaching experience, to guide you through pregnancy and to encourage you to perform safe and effective exercises to improve your health and general well-being.

Now that you are pregnant, and have made the decision to have your baby, you should try from the outset to get healthy and fit, and to remain so. If you look drab, with greasy hair and bad posture perhaps, or if you smoke, you will look and feel terrible. If you project a couldn't-care-less attitude, you will begin to feel most unattractive and resentful towards those close to you.

It is not necessary to spend a fortune or to wear designer clothes in order to look and feel good during your pregnancy; you can look stunning in anything if you are able to achieve a healthy image. Even if you are in a very low income bracket there is no reason why you cannot keep yourself clean and tidy: remember, nine months is a long time and if you start going downhill in the first few months you will probably look and feel a physical wreck by the time you give birth.

So, think positive, and most of all, think *you*!

Jenny Whitby

Part 1

Prenatal Exercise

Why Exercise During Pregnancy?

Exercise during pregnancy acts as a form of preventive medicine which will help to prevent you from becoming lethargic, improve your circulation and generally act as a tonic, giving you a sense of health and well-being.

A pregnant woman *can* enjoy life, she doesn't have to decline all activities just because she is gradually expanding and there is no earthly reason why she should be treated like a 'beached whale'!

You owe it to yourself, your partner and your baby to be in good shape. However, now is not the time to embark on crazy exercise regimes because you've heard that a friend of a friend of a friend did a certain type of class and felt marvellous. You have to be cautious if you haven't exercised for a long time – and there are large numbers of us who come into this category – you must find a class specifically designed for your needs.

Sports such as horse-riding, judo, ice-skating, fencing, hockey etc. should be avoided as should any activity where you might be jostled and pushed or where you might fall heavily. Although swimming is an excellent exercise, avoid crowded pools; keep to the quiet ones or the less busy times, for safety, and swim close to the side in case you develop cramp or get into difficulty.

Remember, the fitter you are before the birth, the quicker you will get back into shape afterwards. If you feel like having a day off, don't feel guilty, rest and then start again as soon as you can. Try putting aside a set time in the day to do your exercises. Wear something you like to workout in, don't settle for an old drab outfit; feel good while you work and convince yourself that this is something you really do want to do: make the effort and don't keep putting it off until tomorrow, unless of course, you genuinely feel unwell.

For some of the exercises you will need a partner to guide and help you; they can also do the exercises with you to provide extra moral support. When we come to the massage section, you will certainly need the help of a partner, you will find it more relaxing to let someone else do the work for you.

When to Start

Start as soon as you feel able to, but if you have any reservations, are very overweight, are extremely tired, have medical problems or if you experience spotting (slight bleeding) check with your doctor first.

Walking is an excellent way to exercise and if you have small children, go for long walks away from traffic and pollution. Take a trip to the park or enjoy a day's outing to the countryside. The fresh air will revitalize you and will do wonders for your skin!

If you are a working girl with a busy routine, do try to set yourself a target date to take a break, work towards it, mark it in your diary and make the escape!

If you have other children and they are still quite young, put them in a baby buggy but make sure the handles are at a comfortable and correct height for you – don't stoop forwards to push. Avoid wearing shoes with too high a heel as this will contract the calf muscles and become very uncomfortable, possibly throwing your back to support your balance. If you can, try to wear flat shoes to gently stretch the leg muscles, which in turn may help to eliminate cramp and elongate the muscles in your back. At home try to walk barefoot as much as possible.

When you become tired, you must stop; don't feel you have to take an endurance test every day otherwise you'll become exhausted and niggly. Remember, you are getting fit to give birth and are not training to run a marathon so adjust your exercise pattern accordingly.

If you are tired when you exercise, your concentration may wander and you could possibly harm yourself, so missing the odd lesson won't do any harm. At the same time, don't make feeble excuses if there really is nothing wrong and you just can't be bothered. Try to summon up some form of enthusiasm. Treat yourself to something which will make you feel good while you exercise – a new outfit, such as a track suit or baggy T-shirt or even a leotard. Once you have spent money on an article associated with exercise, this can act as an incentive to get you started. Gradually, exercise should become part of your daily routine!

When to Stop

Stop exercising altogether if the baby shows signs of poor weight gain, if you have a medical problem such as high blood pressure or diabetes, or if your doctor or obstetrician advises you to stop for any other reason.

If you notice any bleeding during the first three months, do take care. If the blood is brown, it is termed 'old blood' and is usually nothing to worry about. If, however, the blood is bright red or pink, you should be checked as this is 'fresh blood' and could mean a threatened miscarriage. Even very fit, newly pregnant women have to take care and rest if they bleed. The usual remedy is to slow down, put your feet up as much as possible and just let nature take its course; if you do miscarry, it is nature's way of expelling from your body something which is possibly forming incorrectly. Although you may feel absolutely devastated if this happens, you will recover, but it will take time, sometimes months and sometimes much, much longer. Do take advantage of a shoulder to cry on, if you can find one (if not, consult one of the professional organizations listed at the back of the book) or talk to your GP and ask for advice on a support group. Never try to suppress your feelings; you will probably have a lot of sorrow, anger and perhaps guilt knotted up inside you – cry as much as you like. If you are unable to get rid of pent-up feelings, they may, as a result, manifest themselves in other ways as your body can react badly to trauma, eventually affecting your health.

However, if your pregnancy goes ahead, do look after yourself: eat sensibly, exercise wisely – no heavy lifting – and don't take unnecessary risks like running for buses or trains or 'jay-walking'. Appointments can wait but your health can't! Besides, allowances are always made for pregnant women.

Dangers of Over-exercising

Over-exercising is similar to overworking – eventually your body reacts badly to it and during pregnancy you can certainly harm yourself. The purpose of exercising during pregnancy is to give you a general feeling of well-being and vitality, not to take your energy from you leaving you feeling tired and anxious.

If you over-exert yourself, you may experience bouts of dizziness. You could also damage your ligaments by over-stressing the joints. If you begin to feel out of breath, you must stop and learn to listen to your body – do not fight against warning signals.

Body Parts

While you are pregnant, a great deal of body changes take place apart from the obvious 'swelling' of the abdomen. Your posture changes dramatically. Usually the chest is pushed forward and the bottom backwards letting the small of the back take all the strain. Therefore, the body has to be re-educated to keep the lumbar region (the small of the back) 'lengthened'. If this part of the back is not exercised and gently stretched out, the muscles gradually contract and become lazy; this is what causes the dull ache which is so uncomfortable and unnecessary.

Practise 'lengthening' (**Fig. 1**) by standing against a wall with the feet slightly in front of the body. Bend the knees slightly and push the small of the back into the wall until you can feel the muscles slowly stretching out of the tightness. Keep the shoulders down and try not to hold your breath. Hold this position for as long as is comfortable.

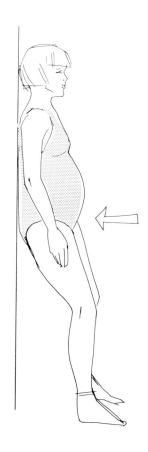

1

As your centre of gravity changes radically during pregnancy, it is imperative that you practise the next simple exercise daily:

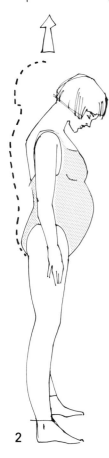

Stand sideways against a mirror (**Fig. 2**), preferably with nothing on, and notice how the back 'sways'. Now try to tuck the bottom under, tilting the pelvis backwards. Imagine the pelvis as a bowl filled with water and by leaning the wrong way, the water will spill out forwards. To avoid spillage, therefore, you must straighten the tail end of the spine to keep it level. Stand with the knees slightly bent until you become accustomed to tilting the pelvis backwards. Only with practice will you perfect this exercise!

2

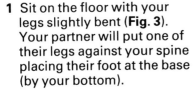

1 Sit on the floor with your legs slightly bent (**Fig. 3**). Your partner will put one of their legs against your spine placing their foot at the base (by your bottom).

2 Lean forward slightly and then come up, straightening your back against your partner's straight leg.

3 Sit tall (**Fig. 4**) and hold this position while your partner slowly moves away; hold for as long as you comfortably can.

This may feel slightly strange to begin with, but eventually, you will feel your spine slowly lengthen and straighten. It is important that you try to relax your shoulders and breathe steadily. With regular practice, you will notice your breathing improve. If you have a tendency to slouch, this should eventually correct itself.

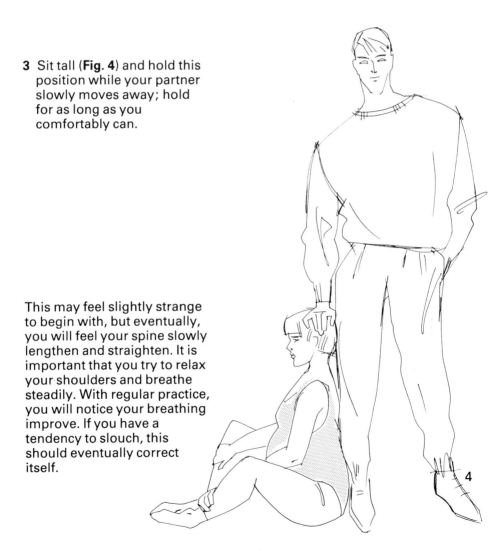

4

Backache

Your back is precious, and during pregnancy, when the ligaments are extremely loose, it is very vulnerable and so you may experience a great deal of lower back pain. As mentioned previously, this is usually due to 'throwing' of the back causing incorrect weight distribution and a hollowing of the lumbar region.

Here is an excellent exercise to stretch the muscles in the small of your back, along your spine and in the back of your thighs:

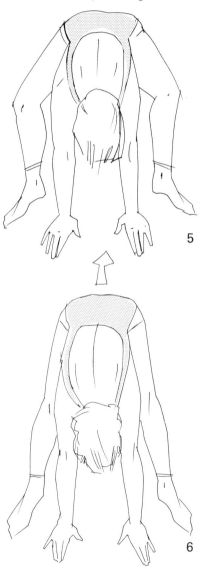

1 Stand with your feet a little further than hip distance apart with the knees turned out and slightly bent. Round your back and drop your shoulders so that they are loose (**Fig. 5**).

2 Very gently, lower yourself and if possible, place your fingers or hands on the floor.

3 Keeping your hands as low as possible, straighten your knees very, very slowly (**Fig. 6**).

4 Hold for as long as is comfortable then bend your knees and come back up to a standing position.

Never lower yourself down with straight knees and a flat back as this causes too much strain to the lumbar region.

Standing: Lean against a wall, with one foot back and one slightly in front. Bend the front knee and rest your head on folded arms (**Fig. 7**). Round your back slightly. If you tuck your bottom under and press the elbows towards the wall, you will feel more of a stretch around the shoulder area and right along the spine especially in the lower back.

When you're carrying out household chores, such as washing up, preparing meals, or answering the telephone, try to keep one knee bent and slightly higher than the other by resting your foot on a low stool or a few telephone directories. This ensures that you are not hollowing your back and straining. Again, it helps to stretch the muscles in the small of your back to prevent them from contracting and causing discomfort.

Try not to slouch; this can age you tremendously and will affect your energy level. Once you get into the habit of standing or sitting incorrectly, bad posture becomes routine and will eventually affect your breathing. Think tall; think light. Straighten your spine by tucking your bottom under and lifting your head so that you feel comfortable without feeling rigid. Imagine you are being pulled upwards by an invisible thread attached to your head. You should feel slightly taller and so much better.

7

Never try to pick up anything heavy off the floor with straight knees as this will put a great deal of strain on your lower back. You must bend your knees (**Fig. 8**) to take the strain in the front of your thighs, gather whatever it is you want to pick up close to your body (**Fig. 9**) and then rise (**Fig. 10**). Once you damage your back you could sustain long-term suffering if it is not properly rectified.

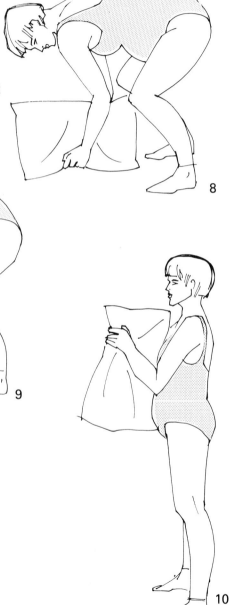

8

9

10

Pelvic rocking: In 'crook' lying (i.e. lying on your back, with knees bent and feet flat), press the small of your back into the floor to stretch the muscles in the lumbar region and abdomen. Breathe normally and hold this position for a slow count of four then release gradually.

To ensure that you are doing the exercise correctly, first slowly hollow your back, keeping your bottom firmly down, and steadily feel the lumbar region come off the floor (**Fig. 11**). Now press this part of your back down so that you can feel it flat against the floor. If you are still unsure as to whether or not you're working properly, ask a friend to place their fingers flat on the floor beneath the small of your back, then press down into their fingers; release slowly so that they can retrieve them!

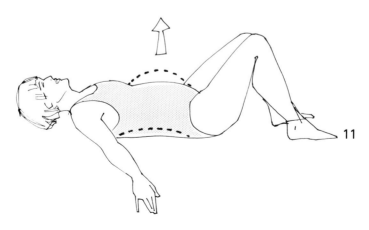

11

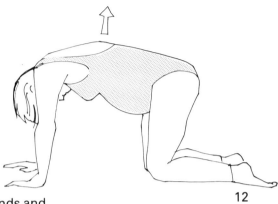

12

Go down on your hands and knees. Place your palms flat on the floor, with the fingers pointing straight ahead to avoid straining the underside of your forearm. Round your back up (see **Fig. 12**) as high as it will go (stretch it the same way as a cat does – head and tail tucked under) and circle it slowly, taking it first over to one side then flatten it, taking care to keep the back flat rather than 'dipping' or 'hollowing', and take it over to the other side (**Fig. 13**). Repeat as many times as you comfortably can and feel the tension being slowly released. Work one way and then the other.

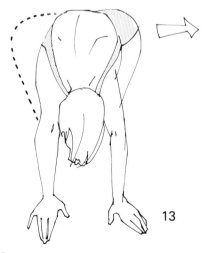

13

1 Hold on to the barre or any other firm surface which feels the correct height for you. Take care not to grip – use the barre simply as a guide (not a life-saver!).

2 Keep your supporting leg slightly bent and bring the working leg up to 45°: don't bring the working knee higher than the hip as the object of the exercise is to slowly stretch the spine rather than to work the leg.

3 Tuck your chin under and slowly lower your head towards the raised knee – not your knee up towards your chin (**Fig. 14**).

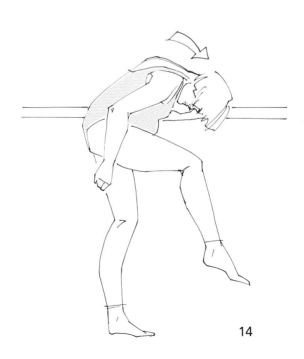

14

If you experience any dizziness with the following exercises, stop immediately, roll on to your side, then on to your hands and knees and stand up slowly. Dizziness can be due to the baby pressing down on the large blood vessels, thereby cutting off the supply to the heart and temporarily affecting the circulation.

This next exercise stretches the back muscles and the hamstrings (the muscles in the back of your thighs) and can be used to relieve 'wind'.

15

1 Lie on your back bringing one knee up on to your chest, keeping the other foot firmly on the floor with the knee bent (**Fig. 15**).

2 Hold underneath (behind) your knee (to avoid strain on the ligaments and joint) and as the knee comes up, breathe out slowly.

3 Hold for a slow count of four, release and breathe in as you lower.

4 Repeat with the other leg.

5 If this position is still comfortable for you, slowly bring up both knees (**Fig. 16**), dropping them out slightly to avoid undue pressure on the abdomen.

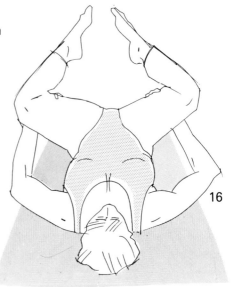

16

Abdominals

In 'crook' lying, place the hands on the tummy and gently pull in these muscles watching your hands lower (**Fig. 17**). Try to keep breathing normally.

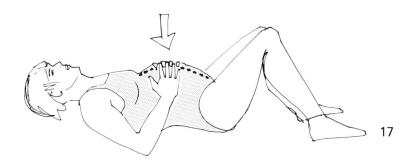

17

Now go onto your hands and knees and either look down at the floor, or alternatively at your tummy. Do not look up towards the ceiling as this will cause you to hollow your back and possibly to strain it (**Fig. 18**). Contract the abdominal muscles breathing in and watch your bulge slowly reduce in size. As you release the muscles, slowly breathe out.

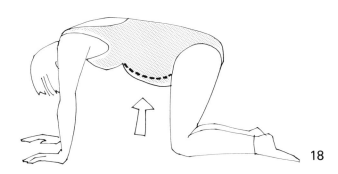

18

Circulation

Sit with your legs uncrossed and with your knees raised slightly higher than your hips. To do this, pile up a few books and place your feet on them; tap your feet as if they're working to a rhythmic beat. This simple exercise will help your circulation tremendously and may help prevent swollen ankles.

Roll a squash ball beneath your feet to improve the blood supply. Roll it along the edges of the feet, beneath the toes, across the soles and diagonally. You can do this as much and as often as is comfortable.

Alternatively, ask your partner to massage your feet. This can be wonderfully relaxing as long as they maintain the correct pressure and, of course, cut their finger nails!

Cramp

You may experience cramp in your feet and calves which may wake you up during the night. A quick remedy, which should give you immediate relief, is to press your thumb into the fleshiest part of your calf muscle. There is a pressure point here so this will almost certainly work. Failing that, here is a simple exercise which should eliminate this painful condition:

Stand with your feet firmly on the floor, and keeping the toes anchored, alternately raise and lower the heels (**Fig. 19**). Try doing this just before going to bed and you'll be amazed at how such a simple routine can help.

19

You should be able to prevent cramp if you avoid pointing your toes; keep the muscles warm (warm muscles are easier to stretch); try not to restrict the blood flow, don't wear socks or 'pop' socks with tight elastic around the tops; and try to drink lots of liquids (especially hard tap water which has a high calcium content).

A few years ago, if you mentioned you were suffering from cramp, you would have been advised to add more salt to your diet. We now know, however, that an excess of salt is bad for us and the intake should be monitored carefully. We only need 1 gram per day but the average person consumes around 10 grams. Salt is particularly high in processed foods, so do read the labels carefully: the higher up it is on the list of ingredients, the higher the content. Salt is, in fact, contained naturally in all fruit and vegetables. However, while you are pregnant, your body may need slightly more than normal. This is because with the increase in body fluids, the salt becomes more diluted.

Massage your calf muscles as much as possible, but if you suffer from varicose veins, never, never rub them as you may 'push' the clot upwards.

Wear elastic tights and roll them on before getting out of bed in the morning. This will prevent fluids from gathering around the ankles and in the feet, and will also help the venous flow (blood returning to the heart). Thick tights can be a problem in the summer when you feel so hot and sticky but elastic hose and also elevating the feet seem to be the only answer. If you suffer from swollen ankles, raise the foot of the bed using a couple of bricks or books (one each side).

Squatting

Make sure you are warm before starting these exercises to avoid straining your muscles and ligaments.

If you have a slight prolapse (i.e. dropping of the uterus), don't attempt the squatting exercises and if you have weak ankles or haven't been in the habit of squatting, don't set your sights on giving birth in this position! Remember, the ankles and knees are taking a lot of strain and unless they are strong, you could be expecting rather too much from your unworked joints. However, squatting is an extremely good way of stretching the inner thigh (adductor) muscles so do persevere. Always lower yourself gently and *never* bounce or you could tear the muscles or ligaments which will not only be very painful, but will also defeat the whole exercise since the only remedy then is to rest!

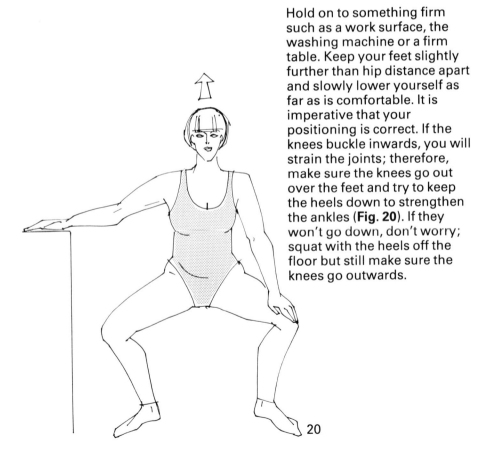

Hold on to something firm such as a work surface, the washing machine or a firm table. Keep your feet slightly further than hip distance apart and slowly lower yourself as far as is comfortable. It is imperative that your positioning is correct. If the knees buckle inwards, you will strain the joints; therefore, make sure the knees go out over the feet and try to keep the heels down to strengthen the ankles (**Fig. 20**). If they won't go down, don't worry; squat with the heels off the floor but still make sure the knees go outwards.

20

If squatting is too difficult for you, stop and carry on with the floor exercises for the inner thigh (see p. 30). If on the other hand you find that squatting is easy, let go of the surface you are holding on to, put your palms together and gently prise your knees out (**Fig. 21**). Hold for as long as is comfortable and then release and rise slowly.

21

Now work with a partner:

1 Again have your feet slightly further than hip distance apart.

2 Hold on to your partner's arms just below the elbows and without gripping or pulling against them, slowly lower yourselves down with the knees out as far as possible. Make sure you keep your bottom tucked under to obtain a good stretch (**Fig. 22**).

3 Hold only for as long as is comfortable and then come up slowly.

This will help strengthen the quadriceps (the big muscles at the top of your thighs at the front) and will also stretch the inner thighs.

22

Cellulite

This 'orange peel' appearance usually manifests itself around the tops of the thighs and on the bottom. In order to eliminate it, try rubbing the affected area with a dry brush before getting into your bath and when you get out; make sure you moisturize your skin well to help retain its elasticity. Massage the fatty deposits to break them down and improve the blood flow. Don't despair if you do notice these deposits; they are due to the extra protective cushioning your body produces and are probably only temporary.

However, to firm up the muscles beneath the fatty layer (fat and muscle are quite separate and one never turns into the other), try the following exercises. Remember that working correctly is more important than the number of repetitions so build up gradually. As the leg muscles are quite large, it may take a while before you notice any difference, but do persevere. Over a period of time, if you are exercising on a regular basis, you will see and feel some improvement.

Inner Thigh

1 Sit on the floor with your legs wide apart and back straight.

2 Place your hands behind your bottom and lift up, pushing yourself slightly further forwards (**Fig. 23**).

3 Slowly lower your bottom back down and feel the stretch on the inner thigh.

4 Repeat, gently, and try to lower yourself to stretch even further.

If you begin to feel any strain on your knees, reduce the stretch by bringing your legs in closer together. If, on the other hand, you feel you can stretch slightly more, do so, but when you reach your limit, hold the stretch for a count of four, and go no further, bringing the legs together slowly.

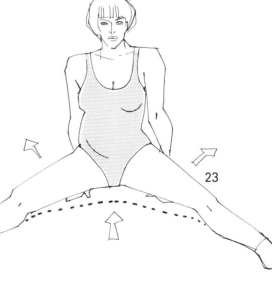

23

Still on the floor:

1 Bring the soles of your feet together holding the ankles rather than the toes (you can stretch further this way).

2 Gently let the knees drop apart (**Fig. 24**).

3 Hold this position for as long as is comfortable then stretch out the legs and start again.

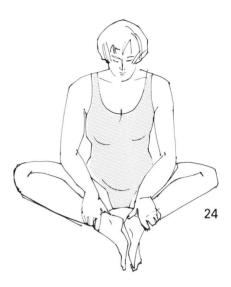

24

Progressing on the above exercise, and still in the same position:

Hold your ankles and with a rounded back; gently lean forward using your elbows to ease your knees further apart (**Fig. 25**).

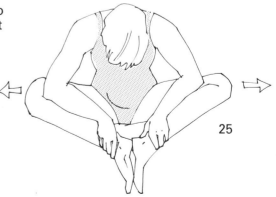

25

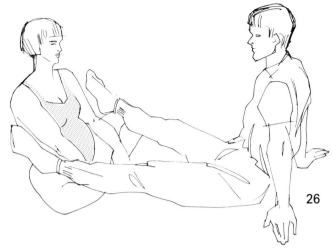

26

For this next exercise take a partner:

Keep your feet together and let your knees drop apart towards the floor. Let your partner place their straight legs over your bent ones. Using the weight of their legs alone, and with no added pressure, they will help to slowly stretch your inner thigh (**Fig. 26**). Again, only hold this position for as long as is comfortable.

Still with your partner:

1 Sit on the floor facing each other, use your hands for support but don't allow your back to hollow.

2 Open your legs as wide as possible and your partner will place their feet against the inside of your ankles to help you stretch out as far as is comfortable (**Fig. 27**).

3 Hold for a count of eight and then release.

The nearer you are to your partner, the more they will be able to help you stretch.

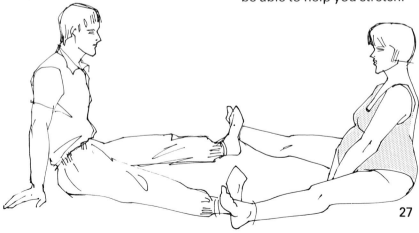

27

If you experience any dizziness with the following exercise, stop immediately, roll over and come up slowly on to your hands and knees.

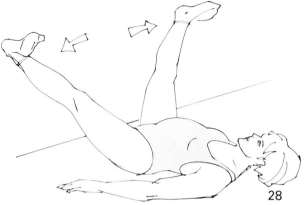

28

1 Lie on the floor on your back with your buttocks about six inches away from the wall; this will avoid putting excess pressure on the blood vessels in the groin area.

2 Raise one leg and then the other and slowly let them fall apart, making sure your back is flat against the floor (**Fig. 28**). Keep your arms down by your sides to prevent 'hollowing of the back'; gravity will assist in pulling the legs out, thus stretching the inner thigh.

3 Hold for as long as is comfortable then bring the legs back together.

To lower yourself from this position:

1 Bend your knees onto your chest and bring both arms into the chest.

2 Roll on to your side bringing the arms and knees down together (**Fig. 29**).

3 Slowly go over on to all fours and come up gently.

29

Sit on the floor with one leg outstretched and the other one bent outwards with the foot resting just above the straight knee. Try to push your bent leg towards the floor (**Fig. 30**). You should feel this in the 'saddle bag' area of your leg as well as in the inner thigh.

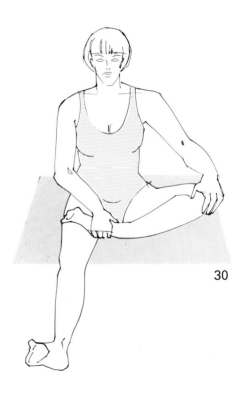

30

1 Make sure your back is straight: neither hollowed nor rounded into a slouch. Sit on your heels with your knees as wide apart as is comfortable – heels turned out, big toes touching (**Fig. 31**).

2 If this is too difficult, take your weight forward, use your hands for balance and lower your bottom down gradually towards your heels as far as is comfortable (**Fig. 32**).

3 To improve on this position and to give a complete stretch to the inner thigh as well as stretching the muscles across the back (*latissimus dorsi*) stretch your arms out in front keeping your bottom as close to your heels as possible (**Fig. 33**).

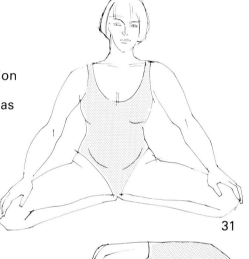

31

32

33

1 Stand with your legs wide apart and your feet turned out and make sure that your knees are angled over your feet when you stretch.

2 Bend one knee making sure it doesn't go beyond the foot to avoid straining the knee joint and ligaments, remember, your ligaments are very loose while you are pregnant due to your changing hormones.

3 Slowly stretch one way and then the other keeping the heels firmly on the floor making sure you don't lean forward. Keep your hips facing squarely to the front and don't twist (**Fig. 34**).

34

Firming the Inner and Outer Thigh

Try the following exercises with a partner and for comfort, make sure you both remove your shoes:

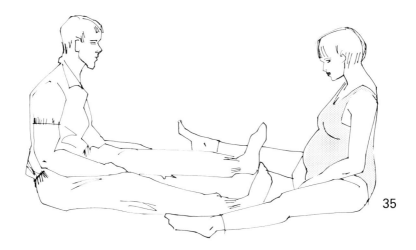

35

1 Sit with your legs outstretched facing your partner.

2 Place your legs on the outside of your partner's with your feet just above the level of their knees.

3 Round your back slightly, but don't round it so much as to put pressure on your abdomen.

4 Use your hands for support and gently push your legs against each others'. The outer pair of legs will push inwards and the inner pair of legs will push outwards (**Fig. 35**).

5 Hold the stretch for as long as you both comfortably can and then release.

Throughout the exercise, breathe normally.

Barre Exercises

These exercises can be carried out equally as well holding on to the back of a firm chair (i.e. a chair which is not on castors and which is not rickety) or alternatively a table. Make sure when you hold on to your firm surface, that your hands are not tensed (to avoid any stress in the neck and shoulders) and that the other hand and arm are relaxed.

Outer Thigh

1 Flex the whole leg, tightening up the thigh muscles and knee joint.

2 Flex the foot upwards to stretch the calf muscle but don't 'turn out'; keep your feet facing straight ahead and try not to lean towards the barre.

3 Lift your straight leg out to the side and lower (**Fig. 36**).

   Try eight lifts or more depending on how comfortable you feel then work the same amount on the other leg. When carrying out this exercise, you will feel a certain amount of tension in the supporting leg.

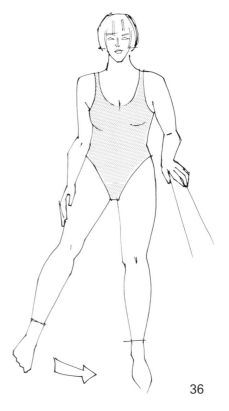

36

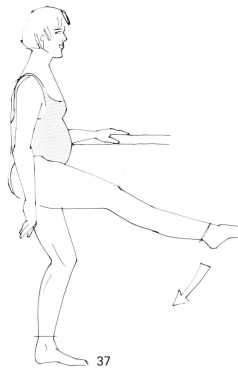

37

Front Thigh

1 Stand with the supporting leg very slightly bent.

2 Point the toes of the working leg.

3 Flex the knee to straighten it and slowly raise and lower it (**Fig. 37**). As well as working the thigh muscles, you are also working the big muscles in your bottom (*gluteus maximus* and *medius*).

Again, try eight repetitions and then swap legs. Increase or decrease depending on your own fitness level, but do try not to give up after the first one!

Back of the Thigh/Bottom

Flex the foot, knee and thigh of the working leg. Without leaning forward or turning your foot outwards, raise the leg backwards, clenching the muscles in the bottom as tightly as possible (**Fig. 38**). Again, do this exercise slowly, avoiding jerky movements. The tightness of the buttocks will determine how high the leg can be lifted and will also restrict movement, thus avoiding hollowing the back. You should not feel any strain in the small of the back; if you do, stop immediately.

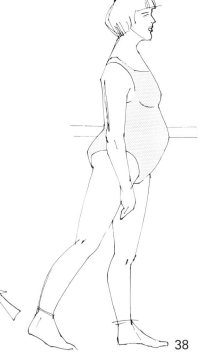

38

39

Hip Rotations

Standing straight, lift one knee towards the chest (*not* the chest towards the knee) and then lower (**Fig. 39**). Now lift the bent leg out sideways (**Fig. 40**). This helps to mobilize the hip and knee joints as well as helping to stretch the muscles in your back.

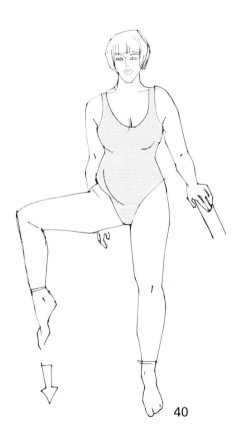

40

Thigh/Bottom

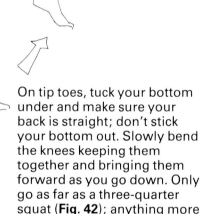

Bend your supporting leg slightly and tense the muscles in your bottom tightly. Bring your other knee up so that it is more or less level with your hip joint and, by tightening up the muscles in the top front of your thigh (quadriceps), slowly straighten your leg taking care not to let the knee drop as it straightens. It doesn't matter how high you actually take the leg but it does matter that the knee straightens! (**Fig. 41**).

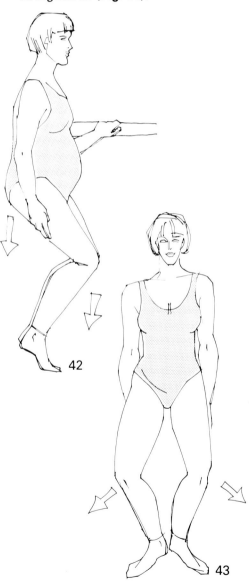

On tip toes, tuck your bottom under and make sure your back is straight; don't stick your bottom out. Slowly bend the knees keeping them together and bringing them forward as you go down. Only go as far as a three-quarter squat (**Fig. 42**); anything more in this position will strain the knees.

This time keep your heels down and again keep the bottom tucked under. Make sure your feet are turned out comfortably with the heels close together. Slowly bend turning the knees out over the feet (**Fig. 43**). This exercise is excellent for strengthening all the thigh muscles and for toning up the bottom.

42

43

– 41 –

Bottom

Keep your heels down with your feet a little more than hip distance apart. With your bottom tightly tucked under, slowly bend the knees out, making sure your back is straight. Feel your buttocks tighten as you bend. It is important that your knees don't buckle and that you don't stick your bottom out (**Fig. 44**) otherwise you will lose the stretch.

44

Imagine you have a sheet of paper between your buttocks and you are gripping to stop it falling on to the floor (for maximum effect, imagine it's a bank statement or tax bill!). Tense the muscles in your bottom making them contract as tightly as you possibly can.

Hold for a count of eight then release. You can perform this exercise virtually any time, anywhere: preparing meals, standing in queues, at board meetings, filing, etc. Wear a skirt or frock though to avoid people noticing a twitching bottom!

Climbing stairs (**Fig. 45**) is an excellent exercise for the thighs and bottom, but if you don't use stairs regularly a low, solid bench will do:

With your bottom tucked under and your back straight, step up with one foot then bring up the other (**Fig. 46**). Now step down, one foot at a time. Try four repetitions on each leg and progress gradually working up to as many as is comfortable without making you breathless. The slower you work at this particular exercise, the more beneficial it will be. However, if it is too strenuous for you, omit it from your routine.

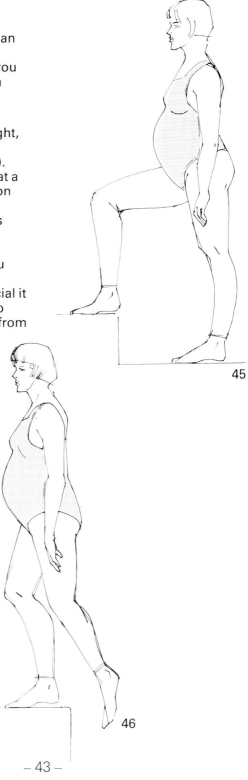

45

46

Sitting and Kneeling

Throughout these exercises, try to keep breathing normally; you should never contract a muscle and hold your breath at the same time as the two combined can impede the blood flow to the heart. If any of the exercises become a strain, stop.

1 Sitting down, make sure your knees are slightly higher than your hips (either rest your feet on a few telephone directories or alternatively, place your feet on tiptoes).

2 With shoulders down and feet slightly apart, press your knees together hard feeling your thigh muscles tighten up (**Fig. 47**).

3 Hold for a count of four and then relax.

Repeat as many times as you comfortably can.

In the same position:

1 Tighten the muscles in your buttocks as hard as you can and feel yourself rise up.

2 Relax the shoulders but don't drop them forward.

3 Push the small of your back into the chair and keep breathing normally.

4 Hold this position for a count of four and then slowly release.

47

The following exercise will firm up the front of the thigh and improve mobility of the knee joint:

1 Sit on a surface preferably where both feet are off the ground, for example a table.

2 Keep both cheeks of your bottom firmly anchored and by flexing the foot and front of the thigh (quadriceps), slowly straighten the leg (**Fig. 48**).

3 Hold for a count of four and then gently release.

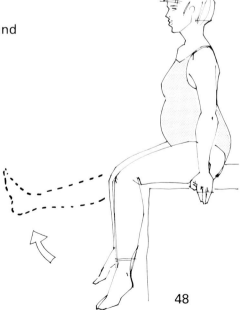

48

Sitting tall on a chair or on a bench, relax your shoulders and hold your hands beneath one slightly turned out knee. Keep your elbows bent to take the strain off your back (**Fig. 49**) – if you straighten your arms, you will begin using the muscles in the back and shoulders and could strain them. Lift and slowly straighten out your leg to the side (**Fig. 50**) feeling the stretch both at the back (hamstrings) and front (quadriceps) of your thigh. Hold for a count of four then bend and start again on the other leg.

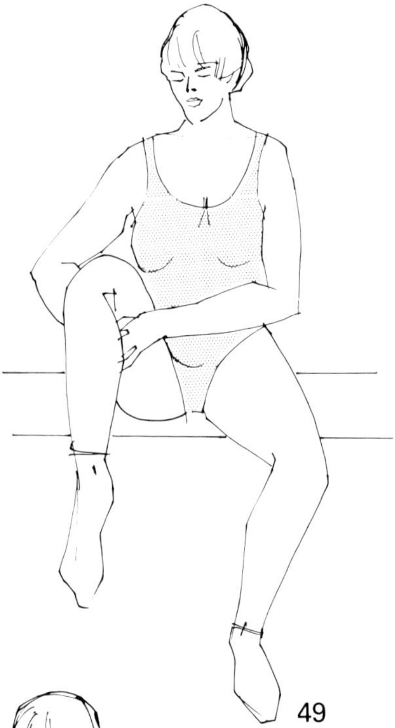

49

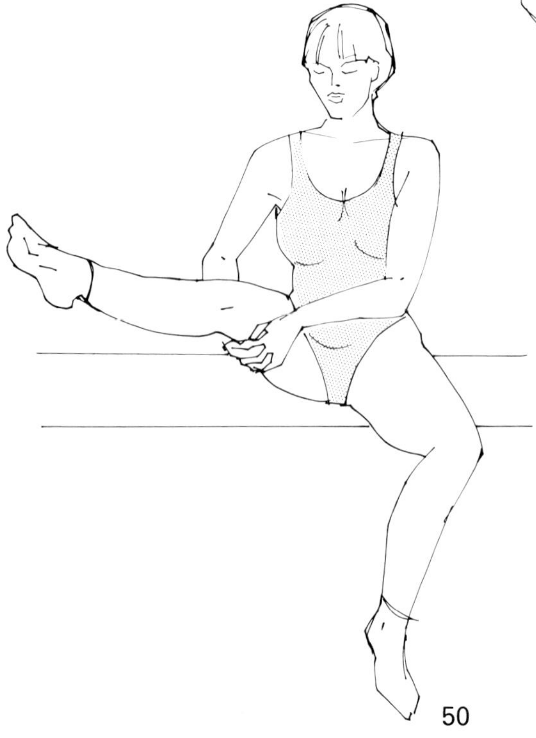

50

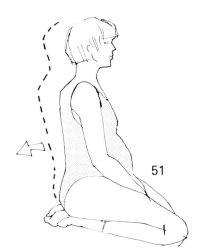

Kneel down resting your bottom on your heels and gently lean back as far as is comfortable (**Fig. 51**). This will help to stretch the front of your thighs and strengthen the knee joint. To increase the stretch (if this is too easy), part your feet and try to lower your bottom between your heels (**Fig. 52**).

Do not attempt the progression exercise if the first one is stretching your thigh to its limit.

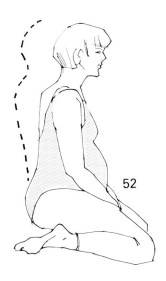

The following exercise makes the muscles work against resistance (as one group of muscles push inwards, others push outwards) to firm the inner and outer thigh muscles:

1 Sit with your knees bent and the soles of the feet touching.

2 Put your hands together and press the elbows into the thighs just above the knee and try to pull the knees inwards breathing out (**Fig. 53**).

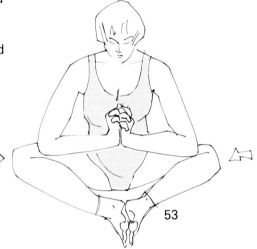

53

3 Now put your hands on the outside of the knees pulling the hands inwards and pushing the knees outwards while breathing in (**Fig. 54**).

Start with four repetitions in each direction and increase gradually.

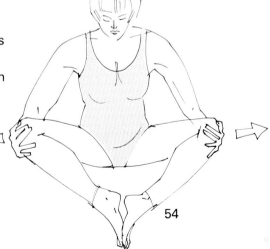

54

Waist

1 Sit cross-legged on the floor on your pubic bones. To do this, sit on one hand and pull back the fleshy part of the bottom, then do the same on the other side.

2 Straighten your back and pull in the abdominal muscles.

3 Place the thumb of your left hand on the floor between the buttocks (try not to take it further as it might encourage you to 'hollow' your back) and place your right hand on your left knee.

4 Slowly twist around to your left side looking over your shoulder, and breathe out slowly (**Fig. 55**).

5 Return to the middle, breathing in.

6 Twist to the right and breathe out again slowly.

7 Return to the middle breathing in.

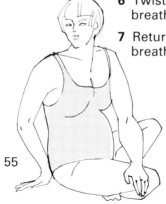

55

Make sure you keep both of your buttocks firmly on the floor as this will ensure a safe twist and prevent you from straining.

Feet, Ankles and Calves

Rotate your feet as much as possible to improve the circulation and to keep your ankle joints flexible.

Sit on a chair with one foot off the floor. Without moving the leg from the knee up, and by working the ankle and toes, try to write your name. This may seem simple enough, but if you actually place a pen between your toes and try to write, you will find it quite difficult. It is, however, an excellent way of working the joints and stretching tired muscles, so do try to practise regularly.

1 Stand at arm's distance from the wall.

2 Keep your heels on the floor and slowly, making sure you keep your back very straight and your bottom tucked under, bend your elbows outwards to lower your body towards the wall breathing out (**Fig. 56**).

3 Hold for a count of two and then slowly come back up, breathing in.

You should feel the stretch mainly in your calf muscles and also in the tops of your arms.

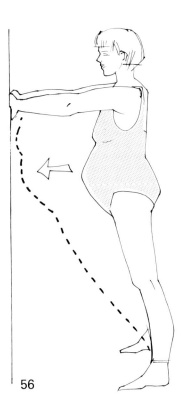

56

To progress on the above exercise and to stretch the upper part of your leg and bottom more, bend one knee up towards your chest and lower yourself as before (**Fig. 57**). Again hold for a count of two and slowly come back up. Make sure your back is straight.

57

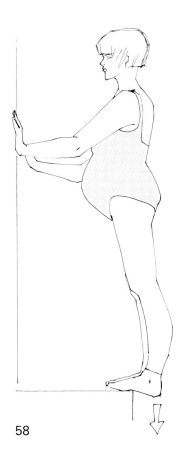

58

Stand on a step or stair or even a thick book and gently let your heels drop lower than your toes (**Fig. 58**). This stretches the calves and is particularly beneficial if you are used to wearing high heels, which tend to shorten the muscles and can, over a long period of time affect your posture.

Arms and Pectorals

Lifting and carrying your baby, quite possibly at the same time as preparing a meal or attending to numerous other chores, will take its toll on your arms and shoulders so now is the time to try and build up some strength. Don't worry, you won't end up muscle bound, just toned up and with a lot less flab hanging on the underarm (triceps) which can look unsightly, not to mention ageing!

1 Stretch your arms out to the side at shoulder level with the palms facing upwards.

2 Rotate the arms from the shoulder joints turning a full 180° so that the palms are again uppermost (**Fig. 59**).

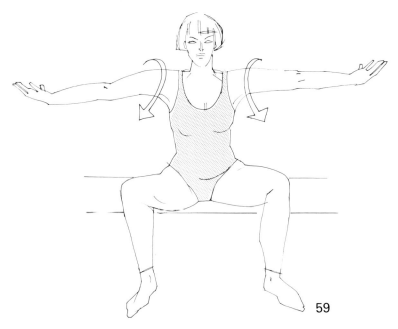

59

This exercise works the whole of the upper arm and shoulder girdle. Try not to 'hunch' your shoulders or lean forwards.

1 Sit tall on the floor, cross-legged.

2 Stretch one arm up to the ceiling.

3 Bend the elbow dropping the hand down your back.

4 Use the fingertips to walk it down even further and to assist the stretch, put the other hand on the working arm just above the elbow and slowly push it downwards (**Fig. 60**).

60

1 Kneel or sit in any comfortable position.

2 Raise one arm with the elbow bent so that the hand slides down your shoulder.

3 Bend the other arm, elbow-downwards with the hand coming up.

4 Try to interlock your fingers (**Fig. 61**).

This might be difficult at first so hold a tea towel or something similar and walk the fingers up to gradually improve the stretch. You will probably notice that one side is slightly more flexible and stronger than the other; this is perfectly normal as you have approximately 10 per cent more flexibility on one side of your body.

61

1 Sit comfortably with the small of your back lengthened to prevent 'hollowing'.

2 Place your palms together in a 'praying' position then raise them up to eye level.

3 Bring the elbows together and gently lift your arms as high as is comfortable (keeping the elbows touching), breathing in (**Fig. 62**).

4 As you lower your arms (keeping the elbows touching), breathe out. You may find that the elbows have a tendency to part so do try to concentrate on keeping them together to work the upper arms effectively. Try four repetitions to begin with and gradually increase. Rest and then carry on to the next exercise.

62

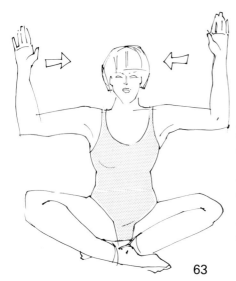

63

Again, sit tall (you may be tempted to hollow your back if you stand). Keeping the arms up as high as is comfortable, with palms and elbows together, with the hands parallel to the elbows, part your arms and take them out to the sides breathing in (**Fig. 63**). As you bring them back together, breathe out.

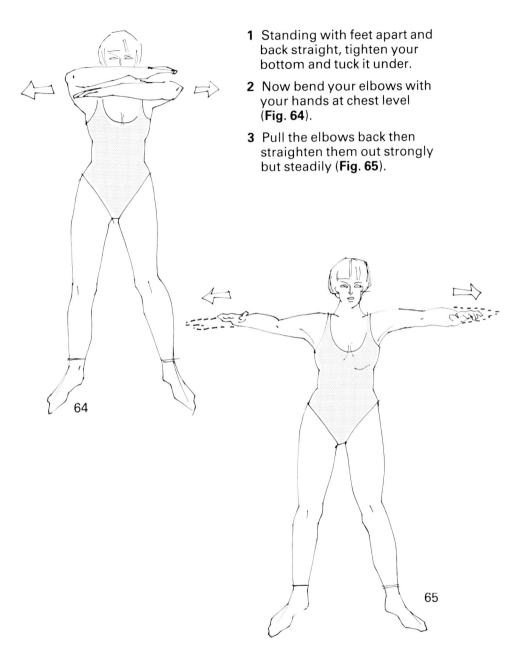

1 Standing with feet apart and back straight, tighten your bottom and tuck it under.

2 Now bend your elbows with your hands at chest level (**Fig. 64**).

3 Pull the elbows back then straighten them out strongly but steadily (**Fig. 65**).

64

65

Repeat as many times as you comfortably can and when you've finished, drop the arms and slowly rotate the shoulders back.

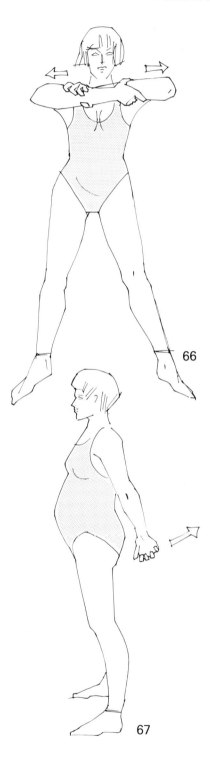

1 Stand with your bottom tucked under and knees loose.

2 With elbows bent up to chest level hold both wrists and gently but firmly, push imaginary sleeves up towards the elbows (**Fig. 66**).

Try eight repetitions, rest and then try another eight.

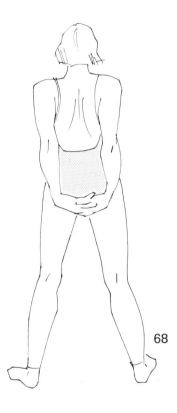

66

68

67

Keeping the back straight (**Fig. 67**), clasp your hands behind your back. Keep the elbows straight and slowly move the shoulders backwards, pushing the chest out. Try to get the shoulder blades to touch (**Fig. 68**).

Sit tall (as you may hollow your back if you stand). Place the backs of your hands in the small of your back. Slowly slide your hands up between your shoulder blades keeping the little fingers of both hands touching (**Fig. 69**). When you can go no higher, try to close your hands bringing both palms together (**Fig. 70**). This does take practice and it may take several attempts before you perfect the exercise.

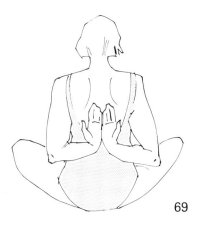

69

70

Breasts

If you are considering whether you would like to breastfeed your baby, but think your nipples may be too retracted, ask your doctor to examine you. You may be advised to wear a breast shield which should help the nipple to protrude and this will be given to you at the clinic.

The following simple exercise may help but do check with your doctor or midwife first so that they can ensure that you are, in fact, performing it correctly:

Using the index fingers on both hands, or index finger and thumb of one hand, gently pull the dark skin of the nipple back towards the body, first horizontally and then vertically (**Fig. 71**), but make sure you don't pull too hard!

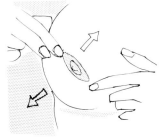

71

Try brushing your nipples every day with a soft brush such as a make up 'blusher' brush to help harden them. Also, massage your breasts every day with vitamin E oil to keep the skin soft and supple, possibly helping to prevent stretch marks.

If you go on holiday, take care in the sun, especially if you prefer sunbathing topless. The melanocyts in the skin (which trigger a tan) are stimulated by sunlight and can react abnormally. If this happens, they may not change back after you have had your baby. The reaction could involve the darkening of the skin areas around your nipples and lina nigra (the dark line, running from the navel to the pubic area, which usually appears in pregnancy). Other areas can also be affected, such as the top lip and cheek bones.

Do make sure you are wearing a comfortable bra, even if you've never bothered with one previously, as this will help to prevent your breasts from 'sagging'.

Getting up off the Floor

You might think the most obvious and the easiest way is to lean back on one arm and push yourself up, but raising yourself this way could damage your back. The correct way is to:

1 Roll on to your side (**Fig. 72**).

2 Come up onto the hands and knees (**Fig. 73**).

3 Bend one leg up first, then the other.

4 Slowly, keeping the knees bent, raise yourself.

72

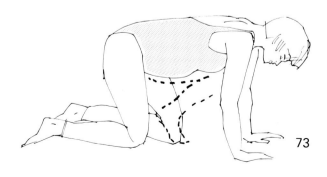

73

Getting out of Bed

1 Roll over on to your side.

2 Drop one leg over the edge of the bed and then the other.

3 Use your arm to lever yourself up.

4 Stand up slowly to avoid dizziness.

Getting out of the Bath

You may experience difficulty in getting yourself up and out of the bath. Gravity will tend to pull you back down and you will be tempted (unless you have 'hand holds' on the sides of your bath), to hollow your back and push yourself, tummy first, upwards. Instead, do as follows:

1 Pull the plug out.

2 Try to roll over on to all fours.

3 Rise up slowly as if you were getting up off the floor (as above).

This sounds difficult, but it is possible. This way, there is no likelihood of you injuring yourself and in particular your back.

Sleeping Positions

Try not to lie with one leg resting on the other as this could restrict your circulation and you may be woken from your sleep with terrible cramp. Lie with the underneath leg straight and the top leg bent over it. (This a good alternative if you have been used to lying on your tummy in your pre-pregnancy state.)

You may feel more comfortable with the top leg slightly raised, in which case place a pillow beneath the bent knee (**Fig. 74**).

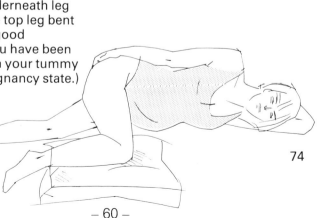

74

Tension

Neck and Shoulders

You may well find you have many problems which sometimes escalate out of all proportion, leaving you in a permanent state of panic which is the last thing you need. You are probably concerned about your present size, and may wonder: 'Will I ever return to my former shape? Will I ever see my feet again?' You may feel slight resentment when you notice slim women, and when you hear small babies crying their heads off you will worry as to whether you will cope. The answer to all these questions is: 'Of course you will.' You may need a little convincing, but in your heart of hearts you know you are perfectly capable of virtually anything.

However, once your imagination propels itself, problems do seem to intensify. Try to stop for a moment, close your eyes. What position are your hands in? Are they clenched? If so, this can lead to a build-up of tension in the neck and shoulder areas. The muscles become tight and hard and feel slightly bruised if touched. In clenching the fists, the muscles in the arms contract and the tension travels up into the neck which brings the shoulders closer and closer towards your ears.

Tense your fists by clenching them for a few seconds. Bend your elbows, and tighten up the muscles in your shoulders. Feel the tension (**Fig. 75**). This is wasted energy, now get rid of it and, for a few minutes, try to relax: drop your shoulders and unclench your fists. Slowly rotate your shoulders backwards and feel the wonderful sensation of tension slowly disappearing.

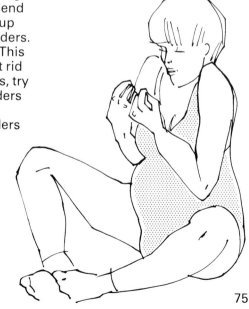

75

Arm circles:

1 Keep your back straight with your bottom tucked under.

2 Circle the arms backwards brushing your ears as you bring your arm up and breathe in (**Fig. 76**).

3 Take the arm back as far as is comfortable without twisting from the hips and as it comes down, breathe out.

Try eight to begin with and increase slowly. If you find the stretch too great, keep the hands on the shoulders and rotate backwards in this manner instead.

Keeping your hands loose and by your sides, lift and bring the shoulders forwards then lift and drop them backwards (**Fig. 77**). Try eight repetitions in each direction.

Only *after* you have loosened the shoulders should you start work on the neck. If you have a lot of tension, this is where it will settle and if you go straight to work on cold muscles in the neck, they may pull and be damaged. Slowly rotate your head and draw a circle with the forehead as opposed to the chin to avoid dropping the head too far back. Rotate in one direction and then the other (**Fig. 78**).

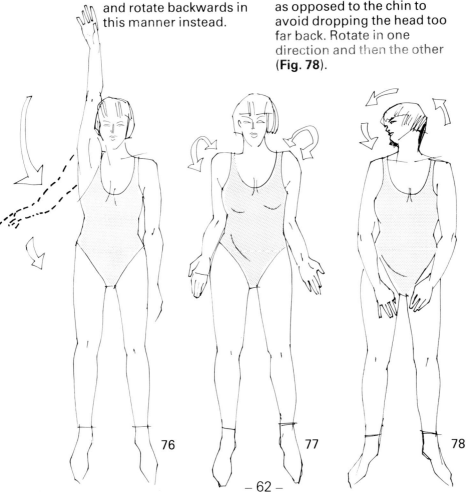

76   77   78

Now drop your head forward on to the chest to stretch the muscles at the back of your neck (**Fig. 79**). Slowly come up, focus your eyes straight ahead and then gently drop your head backwards but not so far back that it results in a 'scrunching' feeling at the base of the skull.

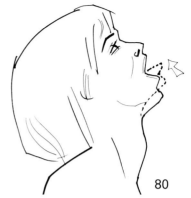

80

79

While you're in this position with your head back, drop the jaw open and slowly bring the lower teeth in front of the top teeth (**Fig. 80**) to tone up the muscles in the front of the neck and to help prevent a double chin from forming – which can happen during pregnancy. Bring your head back up slowly.

Now, move the head to the side (**Fig. 81**), keeping the shoulders facing forwards. Slowly bring it back to the middle (focusing straight ahead to prevent dizziness) and then gently over to the other side.

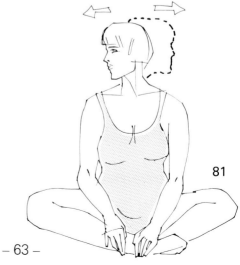

81

Pelvic Floors

This group of muscles is probably one of the most significant in a woman's body yet they are rarely mentioned, even in exercise classes. A great deal of women do not even know where they are or that they exist at all.

The pelvic floors, as the name suggests, lie at the bottom of the pelvis and support the pelvic organs rather like a hammock. There are three openings which are referred to as orifices namely (from the back to the front), the anus – the opening at the end of the bowel; the vagina – extending from the neck of the uterus where you have a show of blood every time you have a period; and the urethra – the passage from the bladder, which is where urine passes from your body (**Fig. 82**). The muscle which opens and closes an orifice is called a 'sphincter'. Each of the three sphincter muscles is joined by larger muscles which form a figure of eight and cross, thus becoming thicker between the vagina and the anus.

As soon as you learn to control these muscles, you must exercise them on a regular basis to avoid embarrassing leakage whenever you laugh, sneeze, run or lift anything. Apart from the leakage, there is always the constant fear of emitting an unpleasant odour of which you may even be unaware.

The area between the vagina and anus is called the 'perineum' and it is here that an episiotomy (cut) is made, if necessary during delivery of your baby (**Fig. 83**). To help keep the tissue of the perineum softer and more elastic and perhaps avoid the episiotomy, rub vitamin E oil into it.

If you have never worked your pelvic floor muscles, you may experience slight difficulty in locating them. They are the muscles that you 'pull in' when you are desperate to find a loo and there isn't one available!

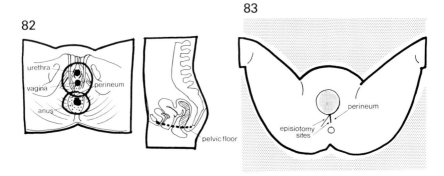

83

82

urethra

vagina · perineum

anus

pelvic floor

episiotomy sites

perineum

Practise *just once* to locate them while you are urinating. Simply stop in mid-stream and pull up hard to stop the flow of urine, hold for a count of eight and then let go. Do not make a habit of doing this exercise while urinating though, as some doctors feel it could have an adverse effect on your kidneys.

An alternative method of locating the pelvic floors is to imagine you are absolutely desperate to urinate, you also have a period and the tampon you are wearing is falling out. To crown it all, you suddenly feel a bout of diarrhoea coming on. There is no toilet available and you are forced to pull all the muscles in hard otherwise you are in danger of losing more than just your pride!

Once you have located the muscles, you are well on the way to a most important exercise routine.

When you first try this exercise, you may find it virtually impossible; don't worry, almost every woman does! You may not be able to feel anything happening at all, but don't give up; you must keep trying. As with anything, practice makes perfect!

Imagine a big inflated balloon has been inserted in your vagina and that by using your pelvic floor muscles alone, you are going to squeeze out all the air. First pull upwards and then pull inwards, expelling every last bubble. When you pull up and in, you should feel the muscles (sphincters) closing and hardening. Even if you feel only a slight sensation in the beginning, it's a start and you will improve.

Try to work the pelvic floors on a 'lift' (elevator) basis. There are three levels to achieve: You will begin at ground level and it is at this point that you will locate the muscles. Once you have got to grips with them, you will take them up to the first floor, hold them and breathe steadily. Now you will take them slightly higher, up to the second floor. They are having to work slightly harder and you will feel the tightness.

Whatever you do, don't let go; it is important that you work a little harder and rise up to the third and final level. You are almost there, so try to pull in just a little more and as hard as you can. This is the biggie and you should feel all the muscles 'sucking' in. Hold on as long as you comfortably can, with normal breathing. You may experience a shivering sensation; this is good and means that you have pulled up as high as you possibly can. Do not worry, however, if you don't manage to feel the shiver; not everybody does (it's a bit like orgasms, some do, some don't!). The important thing is the tight sensation. Now slowly release and let the muscles slide down to the ground floor. Repeat as many times as you can, but try at least eight good, strong ones every day to begin with. You can't hurt yourself or your unborn baby and you can *never* do too many!

During childbirth, the pelvic floor muscles are stretched to their limit and after each child is born, they become slacker. It is, therefore, terribly important to continue practising your routine in order to keep them toned up and strong.

If the pelvic floors are not exercised, your sex life may suffer as your partner will find lovemaking less enjoyable due to your muscles having slackened. Don't despair though, as you can involve and practise exercises on him while you make love! Even if this is the only time you do actually remember to work the muscles, you will both benefit. Aim for the big 'squeeze'. Don't worry about hurting him; you won't and he will encourage you to work harder as this is a very pleasurable experience for him!

If the muscles are not exercised before the birth, they will take longer to function properly afterwards. Once you know how to locate the muscle group, you can begin contracting them literally straight after the birth.

The beauty of pelvic floor work is that you can practise it anywhere, any time and literally in any position. You don't need flashy, glitzy exercise clothes. You can perform the exercises in your best frock, your oldest jeans or with nothing on at all; whilst holding an intellectual conversation or nattering to the postman!

Prolapse of the Uterus

By keeping the pelvic floor muscles working regularly, you can possibly avoid a prolapse (or dropping) of the uterus. As the muscles of the pelvic floor are stretched to their limit during childbirth, they lose much of their strength and it is more difficult for them to support the pelvic organs. Consequently, the uterus may drop. In severe cases, when the exercises have not been carried out, the uterus has to be removed because of the sheer discomfort of the prolapse. So, to avoid unnecessary surgery, keep exercising those pelvic floors!

Breathing

Try to learn the different breathing techniques with a partner so that he or she can 'coach' you during labour. If you both perfect the exercises together, there is less likelihood of you losing control and panicking and you will also benefit by conserving your energy.

Remember, all your worrying will not lessen whatever pain you might endure during the various stages of labour. So read the following exercises carefully and try to familiarize your partner with them too.

Sit in a comfortable position with your hands on your abdomen. As you breathe in, the abdomen should go out, and on the outward breath, the abdomen should go in.

The following breathing exercises, which will prepare you for childbirth, are a method I learned from Betty Parsons, the doyenne of childbirth teaching.

Gentle Breathing – Stage 1

Try to relax completely; make sure you are comfortable with no distractions and consciously try to keep your shoulders down and hands loose with the palms uppermost. Part your lips slightly and breathe in using both the nose and mouth (**Fig. 84**). Do not take deep breaths; just maintain a gentle, steady breathing pattern. On the outward breath, breathe right out as if you are emptying your lungs. Try to regulate your breathing and concentrate on one object, not letting your eyes wander (see mind over matter exercises, page 76).

Stronger/Shallow Breathing – Stage 2

As the contractions get stronger, your breathing should alter. Again, keep the lips parted but don't take deep gasps of air otherwise you might lose control and start to panic (**Fig. 85**).

Concentrate hard on the object on which you have chosen to focus and try to 'ride' above the contraction. As the pain grows, breathe slightly faster and shallower i.e. try not to empty the lungs. As the pain of the contraction subsides, revert back to Stage 1 breathing until the next one arrives. With the passing of each contraction, think of it as being one less to deal with. The one which has just passed, has gone forever and with each new contraction, you are nearer to giving birth. Try to imagine climbing a mountain. Each contraction is a step and each step is going to take you closer to the peak. Come hell or high water, you will reach that peak, hopefully in complete control!

Huffing and Puffing – Stage 3

In the final stages of labour, again, you must focus hard on your chosen object and try desperately not to let your mind wander. If your partner or somebody else is with you, make sure they help you to maintain your concentration. When the stronger, more frequent contractions begin, your breathing will alter. Make a 'ha' sound breathing out, take a shallow breath in; then blow breathing out. With the 'ha', the breath out will be slightly shallower than the blowing. In effect the breathing will be: 'ha', in, 'ha', in, blow out, breathe in, blow out, breathe in (**Fig. 86**).

Relaxation of Body Parts

A certain amount of stress in our daily lives acts as a stimulant and is in fact a good thing up to a point. However, when we surpass our limit both mind and body may suffer. When muscles are tense they can strain, especially when exercising. Relaxation techniques should, therefore, be included in each session to help calm and soothe your mind and body and to give you confidence to cope with difficult situations.

Stress and strain are major problems in our society today and can lead to many heart-related diseases. If you are working and pregnant, you can easily become more worried and tense about extra workloads and deadlines. Your blood pressure will probably rise and you will be forced to rest, perhaps even be hospitalized.

If you are going to be a single mum and perhaps haven't got the support of your family, you in particular need to practise relaxation as you have probably already come up against many hurdles and your mind may be in absolute turmoil. But whatever your situation, you must practise relaxation exercises as much as possible to help in all stages of labour. If you panic when you first start your contractions, you will feel a wreck by the time the baby is born and you will be too tired and exhausted either to listen to or take any advice offered.

Practise this simple routine as often as you can:

Lie or sit in a comfortable position and make sure your surroundings are warm and that there are no distractions. Start by taking a deep breath out and then get into a steady breathing pattern; breathe normally and not deeply. Gently rotate your feet, first one way and then the other. Do the same with your hands and again check your breathing – keep it steady and shallow. If you take too many deep breaths you could hyperventilate and feel dizzy.

Flex your feet hard and feel your calf muscles being stretched. Push down your knees and flex the thighs making them tight and hard. Hold this position for a slow count of four and then release. Gradually feel the tension disappear and experience the feeling of slight heaviness as the muscles relax.

Now do the same with your arms. Clench your fists as hard as you can and watch the knuckles turn white. Straighten your arms and pull your shoulders up towards your ears; hold and then slowly release. Again, don't hold your breath.

Now get to work on the muscles in your bottom and the pelvic floor area. Tense your buttocks as hard as you can. Gradually incorporate the pelvic floors and hold for as long as you comfortably can. Slowly release. Again, feel the tension going out of your body completely and utterly, as if a great weight has been lifted from you.

Take a breather, then tighten up *all* the above muscles: Starting with the feet, flex and hold; then go up to the knees and thighs, keep holding; now incorporate the buttocks, pelvic floors, hands, upper arms and shoulders. Hold all these muscles as tightly as possible for a count of four and continue breathing normally. Slowly release. Let your body relax and feel totally at ease; let the tension slowly drift away.

When you finish this set of exercises, go straight on to the next technique to relax your mind as well as your body.

Relaxation of the Mind

Many people think of relaxation as just closing the eyes and drifting off to sleep. Unfortunately, however, for the majority of us, it is not as easy as this, especially for those of us with over-active minds: Sometimes when we close our eyes, a multitude of problems begin to fill our heads and magnify themselves, causing confusion and tension. It is important therefore that while pregnant, you attend as many relaxation classes as you can to learn different techniques.

If you do have difficulty in relaxing you may find the following exercise extremely helpful. Ask your partner to read the instructions to you and practise as much as possible:

For a moment, close your eyes, and cover them with your hands. Just concentrate on the darkness. Gently place your finger tips lightly on the eyelids and move the eyes from side to side; feel the movement and then stop and feel nothing. Absolute stillness. This is how your eyes should be, in a state of relaxation – with no expression.

Practise the following exercise as much as you can, even if it's only for ten minutes or half an hour each day. In the beginning you may find it difficult, but as with all exercises, you will improve with time.

Take the telephone off the hook, so that you have no distractions and in *all* relaxation exercises always make sure you are warm. If you feel at all cold you will end up using all your energy trying to raise your body temperature, thus making it virtually impossible to relax!

Place a pillow under your head and another beneath the top of your thighs. Lie with your body 'loose'. Let your feet drop comfortably outwards and relax your hands with the palms facing towards the ceiling. Now close your eyes and try to shut your mind off to any thoughts. This may be difficult at first so if thoughts enter, don't elaborate on them, just let them enter and then let them gradually drift out. Eventually you will learn to eliminate these thoughts altogether and 'switch off' completely.

Think of black velvet, soft, dark, smooth, comforting. Feel its softness. Sink deeper and deeper and feel your body becoming heavier and heavier while all your muscles gently relax. Now let your mind drift slowly to a warm summer's day. You are lying on a beautiful secluded beach. The sky is the most fabulous blue you have ever seen and the sun is so bright that your eyes must stay closed, but in a relaxed way. The eyelids are heavy and any frown marks should slowly ease away from your forehead. The sun is warming your skin and a feeling of calm and contentment drifts through your body.

With an outward breath – a big deep sigh – try to empty your lungs, pause for just a moment and then breathe in. Get into a breathing pattern and listen to it. Keep it slow and regular. Concentrate on your outward breath. Slowly drift further and further away from reality. Let the heavy parts of your body sink steadily into the surface it is resting on. The sun is still warming you. The feeling you experience is one of total calm and a sense of being safely cocooned within your own aura. Let your head fall to one side and your jaw relax. Allow your tongue to drop down in your mouth but make sure your mouth is moist to stop your tongue from rising. Let the muscles of your face and neck relax completely.

Feel your eyelids becoming heavier and heavier. Feel your shoulders loosen completely and your whole body become heavy. Maintain this stillness for as long as you are able. You may very well fall asleep. If you do, you obviously need to. If not, just lie there for a while and enjoy the feeling of safety, warmth and tranquillity.

When you are ready, gently wriggle your fingers and toes, then gradually roll on to your side and come up very slowly to prevent dizziness. If you're on the floor get on to your hands and knees first and then rise up.

You can relax equally as well by sitting in a comfortable chair (one which supports the back and where your feet can rest flat on the floor). If your legs are too short, place a few books beneath your feet. Find a comfortable position for your head, place your hands on your thighs with the palms uppermost and go through the motions, as above. You will soon master relaxation in a chair although it may seem a little strange to begin with. With practice, however, it will become as easy as when you lie down. If you are using a chair, it should have arms and support for the head so that when you 'nod off' you don't end up on the floor!

Positions for relaxation

Go down on all fours with knees wide apart and your big toes touching. Rest your head on your folded arms (**Fig. 87**). This is an ideal position for relaxing and you may find it comfortable when you go into labour, it will help take the pressure off your lower back.

87

Again, still with the knees wide apart and toes touching, lean forward and rest on a pile of cushions or big folded blankets keeping the back rounded and shoulders relaxed (**Fig. 88**).

88

Still on all fours, bend one knee up so that one foot is firmly on the floor (**Fig. 89**). This will help to relax your back and will also help stretch your inner thigh muscles.

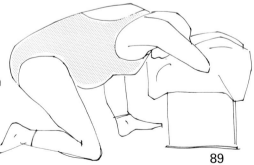

89

Now sit cross-legged with eyes closed. Keep your shoulders down with your hands, palms uppermost, resting on your thighs (**Fig. 90**). Breathe in slowly and fairly deeply through the nose and out just as slowly through the mouth.

90

As with all relaxation exercises, keep the shoulders down and hands loose. If these parts of the body are tense, you will find relaxation virtually impossible. Constantly check, therefore, the position of your shoulders and drop them as low as possible. Feel them becoming heavy so that you really don't want to lift them.

Massage

Massage is a wonderfully relaxing experience at any time, but even more so during pregnancy and labour itself. Physical contact can help to release so much tension.

Encourage your partner to learn the following basic techniques and familiarize them with the type of 'touch' comfortable for you. If contact is too deep, it can be painful and if it is too light, it will 'tickle', thus turning it into an irritating experience rather than a relaxing one! The movement should be slow but definite to help relaxation; if it is rushed, it will simply aggravate you and counter-act any positive reaction.

The majority of tension will be in your shoulders and around the neck area. Make a quick checklist on your body as a basic self-help remedy. Are your shoulders hunched up? Are your fists clenched? Is your forehead tense and with a frowning expression? If so, take a deep breath in through your nose and on the outward breath, through your mouth, try to let go and release all the tension from your body.

Sit comfortably with your hands resting in your lap, palms uppermost and keep your breathing at a steady level. Close your eyes if this helps. When you are ready, ask your partner to start. Massage instructions for your partner now follow:

Start by smoothing the wrinkles from the forehead with a stroking movement of the fingertips, sweeping down to the temple and using a lighter touch, rotating very gently into the temple bone. This should have a very soothing effect. Oils such as rosemary or lavender can be beneficial in encouraging relaxation.

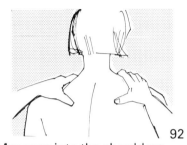

91

Now flatten the palms of your hands on the forehead and pull back towards the hair line slowly and gently in a continuous rotating action (**Fig. 91**). Lastly, using very gentle pressure, run a fingertip across the eyelids, just below the brow, taking care not to pull on the skin as it is extremely sensitive around the eye area.

Now place one hand flat against the forehead to support the head and use the other to work on the back of the neck using all the fingers and the thumb in a gentle but firm 'pinching' movement, pulling up towards the head and pulling down just as the fingers and thumb meet at the end of the stroke.

92

Massage into the shoulders with a gentle 'lifting and pulling' movement similar to the action used in kneading bread. It is in fact termed 'kneading' (**Figs. 92 and 93**). The thumb is used merely as a guide and should not be pressed into the muscle. The fingers should do all the work and always try to massage towards the heart to assist circulation. Work into the shoulder blade with the pads of the fingers as opposed to the fingertips, to avoid digging the nails in; you can use much more pressure over the bone and your partner will tell you if the pressure becomes too strong.
Working over these three areas will certainly help relieve the tension around the shoulders and neck.

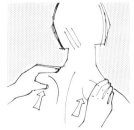

93

Another part of the body which carries a tremendous amount of tension is the bottom, particularly around the sacrum (the bony part of the bottom just above the coccyx or tail bone), to the left and right of the spine where you may, perhaps, find dimples. In this area the pressure of your touch can be increased as you are working over bone as opposed to fleshy muscle and again, use the finger pads (**Fig. 94**). If more pressure is required, use the heel of your hand or the thumbs and press as hard as required.

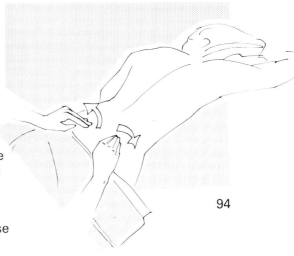

94

The waist and the lower back can also become quite tense and tight. Massage in these areas can bring great relief. This time, anchor your thumbs gently in the waist and use your fingers to work in a circular motion towards the spine and up towards the ribs. Fan your fingers out and rotate. Take care that you are not digging the thumbs in and that you do not pull back on the thumbs as this will drag the skin across the abdomen and may cause discomfort.

When working on the hands, make sure the recipient's hands are uppermost. Ask them to find a comfortable position for their head and to close their eyes to help them relax. Work your thumb into the palm of their hand then steadily work your way into the base of each finger joint and knuckle and then into the fleshy base of their thumb. Finish off by cupping their hand in both of yours and gently pull off slowly and smoothly.

Your partner should now be quite relaxed. But remind her and be aware yourself, of the following 'Mind over Matter' exercises and breathing techniques which she will need when she goes into labour. This way you can be on hand to coach and encourage her when she needs you most.

Mind over Matter

Everyone's pain threshold is different and during labour you will experience pain perhaps as you've never known it before. This will come and go in waves and can last many hours unless you are extremely lucky. You must, therefore, prepare yourself.

A great deal of women do not do this and are not told of the intensity of the contractions. They may learn umpteen positions in which to give birth and be shown how to use the gas and air. They have probably seen beautiful colour pictures of smiling mums holding their new-born babies. They will also, perhaps, see pictures of the baby's head emerging and may have become 'lost' in the wonder of birth. However, labour is not all smooth sailing. It can be very hard work and a real endurance test right up until the first part of the baby emerges, after which the worst is over.

So to save yourself from panicking and going to pieces, you must learn your relaxation and breathing techniques. Don't think that because you have been exercising, you will have a less painful birth. This is not so. The reason for exercising your body is to keep it flexible, to tone up your muscles and also to improve your circulation and heighten your sense of general well-being. Obviously, the fitter you are before the birth, the quicker you will get back into shape afterwards. By exercising regularly, you will learn many positions to help you with your labour, if you are in fact able to move around, but nevertheless, be prepared!

Some women have natural births, some opt for epidurals and some may have Caesareans. If you accept medication or need any form of surgery, you must never, ever feel guilty or a failure – you're not! But whatever type of birth you have, you will find the following advice invaluable in coping with the situation.

Preparing for contractions:
Can you remember back to your school days when you used to play at giving your friends 'Chinese burns'? This is just what you should do now. You may think this totally irrelevant to being in labour, but it's the pain and lack of pain I want you to experience!

95

Sit comfortably with a friend and ask them to give you a Chinese burn. For those of you who don't know what this is, and have never had the pleasure of such playground torments, here is a brief description: Hold your arm out and your partner will hold your wrist firmly in both hands, with fingers close together, one thumb on top, and the other underneath. Then, gripping firmly, they will 'wring' your wrist – quite uncomfortable (**Fig. 95**). Ask them to release when you've taken as much as you can endure!

Now, focus your eyes on one object in the room in which you're sitting. Don't let your mind wander from whatever you choose. Your partner should now give you another Chinese burn. If you are really concentrating and breathing correctly, the pain will seem much less even though your partner is applying the same pressure as before.

You can practise your 'mind over matter' routines in many situations, for example, at the hospital when you need to have blood taken (if you have a fear of needles this exercise will help immensely). If you are tense, the tests become more harrowing as your muscles will contract, your heart will beat faster and you may break out in a cold sweat making yourself feel quite ill. You could quite possibly faint all due to panic. Try, therefore, to be in complete control of your body. Accept the fact that the tests will be carried out (they are not usually quite so bad as you fear), and prepare yourself mentally and physically. You will cope!

Always mention to the medical staff if you are anxious. They will understand and they are much happier if you can relax as it makes their work so much easier.

Don't forget, once you have fixed your eyes on your chosen object, concentrate hard, listen to your breathing and say when you are ready. And remember, practice makes perfect!

Part 2

The Crucial Nine Months

First Visit to the Prenatal Clinic

As soon as your pregnancy test is shown to be positive, your GP will refer you to the prenatal clinic where various tests will be performed. These are nothing to worry about and everything will be explained as you go along. Some hospitals now give you a pre-booking appointment which your partner will also be welcome to attend. At this appointment you will both be guided through all the relevant tests. The talk is usually given by one of the midwives and if you are worried about anything that is going to happen at your check-ups, she/he will put your mind at rest. If you have any social problems, the hospital can put you in touch with the social worker.

Some hospitals are known as 'teaching' hospitals which means that students are trained in the clinics and on the wards and you will probably meet them at your check-ups. You can refuse to have them there at all or you can insist on a maximum number of students present, but do remember, they have to learn and they will be extremely appreciative if you consent to them being there. Try not to worry though, they won't all descend *en masse*; you have the final say and your decision will be respected.

At your first visit to the clinic, which is called the 'booking in' appointment, you will be weighed, your height will be measured and your blood pressure taken – all of this information will be recorded. You will be given a drink of glucose and about thirty minutes later you will be asked to give a urine sample and a blood sample. If you feel queasy at the sight of needles (you are not alone!) ask to lie down; you won't faint while you're horizontal. Having blood taken should not hurt if you relax. You may think this is impossible as you feel yourself coming out in a cold sweat and your heart pounding, but it *is* possible if you practise your 'mind over matter' exercises (see page 76). Breathe steadily and try to release any build-up of tension. Mention to the nurses if you feel nervous or anxious and they will help you all they can. Be in complete control: let them know when you are ready and only then let the performance begin. The nurses prefer you to be totally at ease and will wait for you.

The first sample of blood taken will be the biggest you'll be asked for; don't panic, it won't take long. Just close your eyes or turn your head the other way. The sample is tested for many things: diabetes, syphilis and other diseases or infections, quite possibly AIDS, anaemia, blood grouping, rubella and antibodies screening.

You will also be given an internal examination and for this too you must relax. Try to remember the relaxation breathing (see page 66): in slowly, through the nose, and out, through the mouth. Again, be in complete control and let the doctor know when you are ready. As the examining fingers are inserted into your vagina, breathe out slowly and then practise steady rhythmic breathing. If you are tense, your muscles will contract and make the examination more difficult to perform and therefore more uncomfortable. A cervical smear is usually taken at the same time as the internal examination is carried out. This does not hurt at all – you probably won't even realize it has been done.

You will be asked some very personal questions. This is simply to establish how your pregnancy might progress. For example, have you had any miscarriages or abortions, and if so, how many? Have you had any diseases or infections? Are you married or single? Did you plan your pregnancy and are you happy about it? Is your living accommodation rented or do you own your own home? What is your occupation? Do you intend to continue working?

You will also be asked about your own, your family's, your partner's and his family's medical histories. Is there a history of twins on either side? Are there any hereditary illnesses such as diabetes, epilepsy, asthma or heart disease? You will be asked if your parents are still alive, what their ages are and whether you have any allergies. You will be asked your shoe size (this could be relative to the size of your pelvic opening) and whether you are taking any medication, if you smoke or drink and if so how much?; if you have ever had German measles (rubella) or if you have been inoculated against it. If you have given birth before, you will be asked about the pregnancy and the birth and any complications.

All these questions are quite relevant although you may not think so. Your answers will be treated in strictest confidence. If you don't want your partner to know any of this information, it will not be divulged. You will not be treated differently from any other pregnant woman because of the answers you have given or be discriminated against in any way.

You need to know the date of the start of your last period. If you don't know, the approximate date would be helpful, so try to work this out before your appointment. Was your period normal, i.e. did you bleed for the usual time and was it excessively heavy or very light? You may be asked what form of contraception you have been using.

Your breasts and nipples will be checked and breast feeding will also be discussed. This may seem premature at such an early stage, but some problems can be rectified if need be, quite early on. You will be advised to wear a bra, and if you have inverted nipples you will probably be given a nipple shield to wear which is not too uncomfortable and will help to correct the problem.

As you can see, the first visit to the prenatal clinic is going to take some time and you should allow yourself about half a day. There are lots of questions to be asked and perhaps a few hurdles to overcome, so make allowances and give yourself enough time to recover as you may feel mentally and physically exhausted afterwards.

Blood Pressure

Your blood pressure will be taken at all your antenatal visits and at the first one, the reading taken will be considered to be the 'norm' for you. At subsequent appointments, your blood pressure may drop slightly until, perhaps, the seventh month when it is quite likely to rise a little.

For all your clinic appointments make sure you wear a top – either sleeveless or with sleeves that can be easily rolled up – and which aren't too tight on your upper arm. Having blood pressure taken is not a painful experience, but it may feel strange. A wide band of material will be put around the top of your arm just above the elbow and from this projects a rubber tube with a hollow ball on the end, used to pump up and tighten the band. When this is carried out, you will feel a strong pulsating sensation in your arm which is merely a magnification of your blood pumping. Two readings will be recorded: the upper figure records 'systolic' pressure which is the heart pumping at its maximum level and the lower figure is called 'diastolic' pressure which is the pressure of the heart at rest. The top figure, therefore, will always be higher.

If you have been rushing or feel anxious, your pulse will probably be slightly high, so mention any relevant activity to the nurse before she takes your blood pressure. She may advise you to relax for a few minutes in order to obtain a more realistic reading.

If you are advised to rest because of high blood pressure, take heed and do so. Don't become a martyr – continuing to rush around, fetching and carrying – as you could harm both yourself and your developing baby. Take advantage and put your feet up!

Your Changing Shape & Emotions

During the first few weeks of pregnancy, you may feel many changes taking place but will probably still not realize you are pregnant.

One of the first changes you will notice is the heaviness of your breasts combined with a strange tingling feeling (like icy fingers crawling up towards the nipple) in waves. This can happen more or less straight away. No matter how small your breasts are normally, you may find now that you have to cup them in your hands for support when you first get out of bed.

It is possible that you will feel as if you have the worst pre-menstrual tension ever encountered, possibly combined with terrible headaches and bad stomach cramps. You may notice your waist increasing and your bottom feeling heavier (due to the increased volume of accumulating blood) and you may also feel quite nauseous.

During pregnancy you will feel very emotional and may be very easily reduced to tears. This is perfectly normal and is due to the hormonal changes in your body.

If your partner has deserted you, you will probably feel devastated and cheated. Try to push feelings of anger aside, don't waste your energy in reminiscing about a time in your life which in the future you will put down to experience. Try to have a positive attitude both for yourself and your unborn child and make plans for the two of you.

If you take a break and return to an empty home this can be very distressing. Normally you would probably find something with which to occupy yourself, but while you are pregnant, you will probably sit down and cry your eyes out. Your emotions are in a turmoil and you may begin to wonder if you will manage, but lots of single mums cope just as well as the married ones even though it is usually more of a struggle. You are bound to have periods of loneliness and depression but try as hard as you can to think of your future and that of your developing child.

If you are in a real dilemma, choose one good friend to confide in. If you don't have a good confidante and would prefer to talk to a complete stranger, make an appointment to see the social worker when you next visit the hospital. She will be able to ease your mind and will help you sort out any practical problems. She might be able to put you in touch with other women in the same situation as yourself if this is what you would like.

Try to absorb any advice given to you in a professional capacity. If you are confused by any of the information that is offered, do say so; don't leave in a state of confusion and turmoil; your time is as precious as anybody else's!

Up until about week 15 is a very vulnerable time for your developing baby. Avoid taking unprescribed drugs of any kind, including pain killers, allergy pills, sleeping pills, and cigarettes and alcohol. Also try to reduce your coffee intake. If you suspect that you may be pregnant and you are taking a course of medication, talk to your doctor *immediately* to check whether they could be harmful to your unborn child. Many drugs cross the placenta which means they are absorbed by the foetus, and could affect the development of vital organs and limbs.

If you feel nauseous as soon as you get up in the morning, keep a couple of dry, wholemeal biscuits on the bedside table and eat them before you get out of bed.

If you are suffering from insomnia, check your diet, and reduce the intake of greasy, fatty food eaten late at night. Try taking some of the natural remedies available from homoeopathic or health food stores, but do mention to the sales assistant that you are pregnant. If you are not sure whether or not to take a certain remedy, or if the assistant is not familiar with the product (as sometimes happens), *do not take it* – you have a lot to lose!

Some women feel pregnant virtually as soon as they have conceived, but the only way to be totally sure is by having a pregnancy test. This can be carried out at the hospital by arrangement with your GP or you can do it yourself at home with a kit available from most chemists. Some of these kits can detect pregnancy as soon as one day after your missed period but errors can be made this early. If it is taken at least five days after your missed period, the reading will be more accurate. Always make sure the urine sample you take is the first of the day, and read the instructions on the kit very carefully.

Weight Gain

Weight gain can vary a great deal between women in pregnancy. It can be as little as 10 lbs or much more than the recommended 28 lbs. This depends entirely on your food intake and your body make-up.

Ideally, you should, in the first three months, gain very little, probably between 2–4 lbs; during the following three months, approximately 1 lb per week and by the week of your expected delivery date (week 40), you should not have gained more than around 28 lbs altogether. This may seem like a lot of excess weight, but the majority of it is shed as soon as you have delivered the afterbirth: the baby, the placenta (afterbirth), your breasts and uterus account for around 20 lbs. All the rest tends to stay unless you work hard to dispose of it. Therefore, to prevent excess weight gain, eat sensibly, and enjoy every bite you take. Try not to indulge in food because you are bored, using it as a comforter or eating just for the sake of it, and don't be tempted to binge – you'll regret it when the fat just sits there and refuses to budge after the birth! However, now is not the time to venture into crazy diets which promise dramatic weight loss as you may deprive yourself and your growing baby of the vitamins and minerals essential for good growth and development. If you feel you need to know if you are gaining too much body fat, measure the top of your thighs; the measurement should remain more or less stable throughout your pregnancy, although towards the end you may notice a slight increase.

Amniocentesis

If you are over thirty-five years of age, you will be asked if you would like to undergo an amniocentesis test – an investigation in which some of the fluid surrounding the foetus is removed and tested for possible abnormalities. If you are undecided, you can make an appointment for counselling to discuss the pros and cons in more detail with one of the doctors. You will not be forced into having the test if you decide you don't want to. For more information on amniocentesis, see Appendix on page 128.

The Growing Foetus

Weeks 3–4

You may feel as if you have extremely bad pre-menstrual tension, coupled with a sense of being very bloated. You will probably feel worn out and you may even have symptoms similar to those of the flu. You could become forgetful and irritable. Don't despair; this is perfectly normal and is due to the sudden increase of oestrogen and progesterone levels in your body.

The minute, fertilized egg will have implanted itself in the lining of your womb.

Weeks 4–5

You will have missed your period but you may experience some dark brown bleeding which is in fact 'old' blood. This is quite common. Only if it turns bright red could it mean that the pregnancy may not continue. If this does happen at this stage, you will probably not even realize you were pregnant and your period will just seem excessively heavy. If, however, there is no bleeding, the pregnancy is going ahead.

The embryo is still minute but already the spine is beginning to form.

Weeks 6–7

You will probably have realized by now that you are in fact pregnant and it is important, therefore, to cut out any potentially harmful medication as the embryo is extremely vulnerable.

The spine has now formed and the head will start to grow. Formation of the liver and kidneys is taking place and little stubs known as limb buds are present. The eyelids are also beginning to form.

Weeks 8–9

Start to rub vitamin E oil or cream into your breasts and abdomen to keep the skin supple. This may help to prevent stretch marks and will maintain the skin's elasticity.

Your baby is now about the size of a thimble and nearly all the internal organs are present including the heart which will start beating. The little limb buds are increasing in size and at this stage small bumps appear which will develop into shoulders, elbows, hips and knees.

Week 10

Your waist will have increased with the build-up of extra blood and you may experience bouts of extreme tiredness. Check your posture to avoid unnecessary backache.

The head of the baby is growing steadily and is quite out of proportion with the rest of the body. The face is gradually becoming more defined. The eyes are slowly taking shape and the eyelids have completely formed although they will remain fused together until later on in the pregnancy.

Weeks 11–12

If you have been suffering from morning sickness, it should now begin to ease off slightly and if you have been urinating more than usual, this should also begin to lessen although you may now start to experience slight constipation. Watch your diet: eat plenty of roughage/fibre (there is no fibre in meat or eggs).

If you have eased down on your exercise programme, you should be able to gradually build up again from now on, but do check with your doctor first and keep watching for any bleeding. If there is a show of blood, you must rest. This could be a warning sign for you to slow down.

The baby is beginning to look more human although the head is still quite large in comparison with the body. As the limbs continue to grow, it is *imperative* that you do not take any unprescribed medication which may have an adverse affect on the baby's growth. If you have a scan at this early stage, the sex of your developing child will be uncertain as the external sex organs have not yet completely formed.

Week 14

You are virtually over the most crucial period and your baby will now be able to establish itself as it has almost completely formed. You should begin to feel similar to how you felt before your pregnancy, with more energy and you should feel able to get back into your normal routine.

Start rubbing vitamin E oil into your perineum which is the skin between the vaginal and anal openings. It is here that an 'episiotomy' (cut) will be performed if necessary. The cheapest way of buying vitamin E oil is in capsule form (available from all good chemists). Simply burst the outer coating and using your fingers, spread the oil over the perineum. It might be a good idea to wear panty liners (unperfumed) to prevent the oil from staining your underwear. Loose tissues tend to move around and can end up halfway up your back making you feel extremely uncomfortable!

Week 16

Your baby's eyebrows and eyelashes are beginning to grow and a fine layer of hair called 'lanugo' covers the body. This is when amniocentesis is performed if necessary. Usually this is routine in the UK if the woman is over thirty-five years of age or if there are any complications. However if you don't want the test it is not compulsory.

You will now begin to look pregnant and it is important that you regularly check your posture to prevent straining your lower back. The sex of the baby can now be determined. If you don't want to know this information make sure your request is written on your co-operation card.

Week 18

You should be able to feel your baby moving in all directions as the arms and legs are now well formed, as are the fingers and toes. There are also the beginnings of little ridges for finger and toe nails in the form of a slightly hard layer of skin although they do not develop until Week 24.

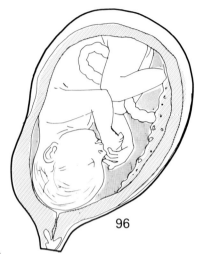

96

Week 24 (Fig. 96)

You will begin to feel the strain of carrying the extra weight of your unborn child. Your legs may feel very tired and heavy so rest as much as you can and try wearing elastic tights. Keep checking your posture and make sure your bra is both supportive and comfortable. The baby will be able to suck its thumb within the womb and the harder layer of skin on the toes and fingers will begin to thicken into nails.

Week 26

Your abdomen is now very stretched and it is important that you continue oiling or creaming the skin both to soften it and hopefully to avoid stretch marks. But don't worry if these do appear, because although you can't get rid of them completely, they will fade after the birth. Continue rubbing Vitamin E oil into your perineum, and keep practising your pelvic floor exercises (see page 64). Your baby should begin to look more 'normal' now as the head is almost in proportion to the rest of the body.

Week 32

You will probably begin to feel absolutely exhausted so rest as much as you can and eat when you can. To avoid heartburn try not to eat late at night or just before going to bed, and don't start 'eating for two' if you become restless or bored. You don't have much longer to go although it probably does seem as if you've been pregnant for an eternity.

Your baby's head is now completely in proportion to the body.

Week 36

You may be feeling very heavy and every step will seem like an endurance test. Stairs, for example, may sap your energy. Rest as much as possible before the birth as afterwards your routines will go haywire! Try to catch up on the reading you have always promised yourself that you will do, or the knitting you haven't quite finished.

If this is your first baby, the head will have engaged and you may have to urinate more often because of the pressure on your bladder. If, however, this is not your first baby, the head may not engage until week 40, so don't panic. If you are having your baby in hospital, pack a small bag ready for taking in with you; don't leave this until the last minute! If you are having a home birth, make sure you are prepared and that the relevant telephone numbers are to hand. Don't forget to arrange baby sitters etc. if you already have small children.

Your baby is now fully formed and if it were to be born at this stage, the chances of survival would be quite high.

Week 40

Your baby has now reached maturity and is ready to be born. However, like trains and buses, they very rarely arrive on time. You might feel less movement inside you. This is because there is now very little space in which the baby can move around, although you will obviously still see and feel the limbs kicking and punching. You will also be feeling extremely heavy and uncomfortable.

Rest as much as you can and conserve your energy. Practise your breathing techniques and your 'mind over matter' exercises (see page 76).

As soon as the waters break, seek immediate medical attention to avoid infection.

Clothing

Of course you're going to feel as though you resemble something similar to a big bear, but luckily, you *can* disguise your changing shape. From the word 'go' you will steadily increase in size. If you have track suits and the waist gets too tight, do not suffer in silence or feel you have to buy new clothes which you may not be able to afford – simply rip out the elastic and put in a draw-string: be comfortable. If you don't have the funds to invest in big shirts or sweaters, borrow them. Being pregnant needn't be an expensive venture and it can be fun – you can get away with so much more fashionwise! Baggy clothes look good; dress them up or down, experiment and feel great.

If you are short of funds, visit the local Oxfam shop or go to jumble and car boot sales. If you choose a good area, you are quite likely to pick up some very good bargains. Invest in a pair of big trousers and keep them up with multi-coloured braces (which cost only a couple of pounds) – these should last you a good few months!

Friends will rally round to help as soon as they learn of your pregnancy so lean on them slightly.

Underwear

Bras As soon as you realize you are pregnant you should start to wear a good supportive bra. Apart from the comfort aspect, you are helping to support the added weight of increased fluid and the muscles and ligaments – the bra will thus prevent your breasts from 'sagging' after the birth. Try experimenting with sports bras, they provide lots of support without the frills and are usually very well designed although some of them can tend to look rather like shoulder holsters. Having suddenly to wear a bra can be a nightmare if you have never had to wear one before, as you can be confronted by so many different styles with wires, foam and lace. Do not buy one just because it looks attractive; ask the assistant to help you. If you go to a good store, you can be properly measured and advised. In many cases, a design may look very pretty, but the lace may itch and the straps could rub. Look for a design with cotton straps as opposed to elastic ones which 'give' too easily. Make sure it doesn't come up too high into your armpit and beware of zips in the cups – these can look quite practical but you may need to be scraped off the ceiling if you catch your skin in them!

Knickers Try to avoid nylon pants, but if you already have them and feel happy with them, make sure they have a cotton gusset so that air can circulate. When buying new ones, choose undies made of natural fibres as opposed to man-made, which will help to keep you cool especially if you are prone to excessive sweating or if you have any discharge. If you do have a heavy discharge, you may emit an unpleasant odour, in which case you must wash yourself regularly, increase your pelvic floor exercises and use unperfumed panty liners!

Tights/Stockings Ordinary tights from your usual supplier should be OK but if these begin to feel uncomfortable, do buy the maternity ones. Some of them do look gigantic but this is because they are designed to go over your bump.

If you are in the habit of wearing stockings but can't find a big enough suspender belt, alter one of your existing ones by sewing in an extra piece of elastic at the front in the middle and another piece at the back.

If you suffer from swollen ankles and feet, or have varicose veins which are becoming troublesome, wear elastic tights or stockings.

Try to avoid any variety of tights or stockings with restrictive tops as these can affect your circulation and become extremely uncomfortable.

Shoes

Make sure your shoes are comfortable; if they don't fit properly, this will be reflected in various ways: your back may suffer and your feet certainly will.

Towards the last few weeks of your pregnancy, you may notice your feet spreading and possibly swelling slightly. Don't go out and spend vast fortunes on new pairs of shoes as your feet should revert back to their normal size after the birth.

Health Hazards

Smoking
Smoking should be cut out completely for your baby's sake. If you smoke, you run the risk of having a smaller baby and one who may be slower to develop and learn. It is becoming more and more socially unacceptable to smoke and particularly in the case of pregnant women. Your clothes will smell, your breath will smell and you may require more dental treatment since your gums become more susceptible to bleeding and possible infections during pregnancy. If you *can* give up, think of the financial benefits.

Alcohol
Alcohol will also affect your unborn child. Especially crucial are weeks 6–12 when the foetus is forming. Obviously, some women are totally unaware that they are pregnant at such an early stage, but if you do have any inclination, you should try at least to *reduce* your alcohol intake: no more than one glass of wine or one measure of spirit or half a pint of beer per day. This may not seem very much, but taken over a week, you can see that it mounts up. An excess of alcohol can cause what is known as 'Fetal Alcohol Syndrome' (FAS) which means your baby could be born with an abnormality such as a harelip, cleft palate or could perhaps have some form of limb deformity.

Don't feel a 'party pooper' for refusing to drink, most people expect a pregnant woman to decline alcohol and respect you for it. You can also become very popular by offering to drive! However, if you really do feel like a drink on the odd occasion, it won't harm as long as you have just one. Try watering down wine with tonic water, it's refreshing and lasts longer, but remember: the measure of wine is still the same – it doesn't lessen!

If you feel you may have a serious drink problem, seek help from Alcoholics Anonymous, whose address is at the back.

Tea and Coffee
Tea and coffee act as stimulants (and caffeine does in fact cross the placenta) so do avoid them. Instead try herbal teas, mineral water, fresh fruit juices or milk.

Medication
Only take medication prescribed by your doctor or by your homoeopath.

Diet: Healthy Eating

Maintaining a healthy diet is essential during pregnancy, although over-eating can turn into a nightmare. You will feel heavy and lethargic and will find yourself in a 'Catch 22' situation: your energy level will drop and you will probably turn to food to console yourself. This in turn can lead to depression and is a difficult situation to escape from. Try to sustain a good, varied diet to include lots of fresh fruit and vegetables eaten raw or very lightly cooked in order to retain as many vitamins and minerals as possible.

Foods to Avoid

Sugar, both white and brown (there is no nutritional difference), glucose and molasses are all to be avoided. Get into the habit of reading labels on soft drinks and canned foods to spot the added sugar and sweeteners. Sugar is classed as 'empty calorie' food and has no nutritional value whatsoever. It does, however, provide instant energy. You may notice this if you eat a bar of chocolate, but as soon as you have reached your 'high', your energy level will drop drastically leaving you feeling more tired and just as hungry! If you need a quick pick-me-up, eat a piece of fruit instead – the natural sugars will release slowly into your blood stream (the same as honey) and you will have the added advantage of the fibre/roughage content which will help to give you a feeling of 'fullness'.

Read the ingredient labels on yoghurts carefully as well. They may be advertised as having a 'low fat' content, but some of the fruit varieties have, on average, four teaspoonful of sugar, depending on the brand. Try to cut down on pastries and biscuits too as they have a very high sugar level and will put pounds on you which will be stored as fat. Fried foods should be avoided to help prevent heartburn. Try grilling, steaming and baking and get into the habit of using herbs and mild spices to season.

If you are trying to cut down on smoking, don't turn to little sweet mints instead; many of these are heavily loaded with sugar, approximately seven teaspoonful in a tube!

The Right Foods to Eat

Basically, you should aim for a good, varied diet, avoiding tinned foods (apart from tinned fish in moderation) and processed foods. If you need vegetables in a hurry, and for some reason you are unable to purchase them in their natural, fresh state, buy the frozen varieties as these retain many vitamins. Frozen peas especially are extremely high in fibre!

Proteins Foods such as meat, fish, eggs, milk, cheese, mushrooms, and pulses such as peas, beans, nuts and lentils are a good source of protein – essential for the growth of your baby and for your own well-being. Even if you are vegetarian, therefore, you can still obtain your protein; the soya bean is extremely versatile and has a high protein content. Other good sources are hard cheeses such as parmesan and cheddar (although the salt content is quite high), cottage cheese, yeast extract, various nuts (especially almonds, brazils, black walnuts, peanuts and pistachios) and wheatgerm.

Fats Although fats are essential in the diet (they can help improve the elasticity of the skin), they should be taken in moderation as they can lead to excessive weight gain (fats, both animal and vegetable, contain virtually twice as many calories as carbohydrates). If you have a family history of heart disease, monitor your intake carefully to help lower your cholesterol level. Fats do, however, provide a certain amount of energy and you will find them in butter, margarine, cheese, oil and lard.

Iron This is essential for the blood and since a high percentage of women can become anaemic during pregnancy they will most probably be prescribed iron tablets. These can, however, cause constipation and if this persists, consult your doctor to see if the dose you have been prescribed is too high. Good sources of iron are offal such as liver (if you soak this overnight in milk, it will take away the slightly bitter taste), red meat, egg yolks, mussels, oysters, mushrooms and many green vegetables especially *cooked* spinach. Iron is also found in dark chocolate (not the milk variety), bran, oatmeal and wheatgerm and lastly parsley (which also helps rid the breath of garlic).

Cooking in an iron pot will absorb iron into your food.

Vitamins You will probably be advised to increase your vitamin intake during pregnancy and the following information will help you identify different foods containing the various vitamins to help you in the preparation of your diet.

Vitamin A This is essential for good eyesight.

It is found in dandelion leaves, which can be used in salads (they are also a mild diuretic), watercress, *cooked* spinach and broccoli. Dairy products such as milk, cheese and yoghurts are good sources and it is also found in liver and fatty fish (e.g. herring, mackerel and sardines), fresh, brightly coloured green vegetables and carrots. Whenever possible, try to select your merchandise yourself, making sure it is unbruised and firm.

Vitamin C An essential vitamin for good clear skin and healthy gums (gums become vulnerable during pregnancy and prone to bleeding). This vitamin is easily obtained and the most obvious source which springs to mind is oranges. However, this vitamin is also contained in other citrus fruits, such as grapefruits, lemons, blackcurrants and also strawberries.

Potatoes, leafy green vegetables, red and green peppers, watercress and *cooked* spinach and broccoli are good sources. Some vegetables, such as cabbage and cauliflower, retain more vitamin C when eaten raw (green cabbage is more nutritious than the white variety). To retain vitamin C in tomatoes, cut them just before using as the content reduces rapidly once they are cut. It is also found in mushrooms, which should only ever be rinsed slightly and never scrubbed or peeled. Always look for firm white specimens; and don't be fobbed off with battered brown ones!

Vitamin D A very important vitamin for pregnant and lactating women.

Sunlight and sunshine on the skin are excellent sources of vitamin D, but if you are in strong sunlight, this can have an adverse effect on certain parts of the body during pregnancy, causing blotchiness which may or may not disappear after the birth, so do take care. However, lack of vitamin D can also have an adverse effect on the body. It has been found that rickets is on the increase especially in Asian communities where bodies tend to be covered for protection against the sun.

Vitamin D is found in butter, margarine, egg yolks and mushrooms.

'B' Vitamins The 'B' vitamins convert food into energy and are usually grouped together. Below is a brief breakdown of the various B vitamins:

Vitamin B_1 Thiamine: this can be lost during cooking and storage. So cook foods lightly, trying to keep vegetables slightly crunchy, which is also good for your teeth. If you eat a large number of carbohydrates, you need to increase your thiamine intake to metabolize them. Thiamine can be found in low fat milk, enriched flour, pulses, meat, poultry and yeast.

Vitamin B_2 Riboflavine: this can be destroyed by storing in direct light (which also has a tendency to 'sour' certain foods). If you do not drink milk you will have a deficiency of this vitamin and will quite possibly be prone to minor ailments such as chapped lips and perhaps bloodshot eyes. Riboflavine can be found in cheese, eggs, fish, kidney, leafy green vegetables, liver, milk and yeast.

Vitamin B_3 Niacin: this is found mostly in milk and eggs. A lack of this vitamin can cause you to become nervous, irritable and depressed.

During your pregnancy you should be aware of your intake of B_3 as your emotions are so erratic.

Vitamin B_6 Pyridoxine: women who are pregnant need this vitamin. If you suffer from a deficiency of B_6, you can become terribly depressed, tired and sometimes anaemic. B_6 can easily be destroyed when food is heated or processed so try to eat a well-balanced diet to include lots of fresh fruit and freshly squeezed fruit and vegetable juices.

Folic Acid Some pregnant women show a deficiency of folic acid which can lead to extreme tiredness and depression.

It can be found in yeast and yeast extract, *cooked* spinach, peas, broccoli, almonds, hazelnuts, peanuts and bran. It can also be found in raw Brussels sprouts (which are not as bad as they sound) as well as in cabbage and avocados.

Uncooked fresh vegetables should be included in your daily diet whenever possible. Experiment with different types of salads which needn't consist solely of the proverbial lettuce leaf and well-worn tomato. Use a base of fresh watercress and parsley and add bean sprouts, kiwi fruit or any other fresh fruits of the season, adding toasted poppy or sesame seeds. Try using yoghurt and honey as bases for your dressings.

Calcium We are told from an early age that calcium is good for strong teeth and healthy bones, but it also helps in calming the nerves, relieving leg cramps, insomnia and nervous exhaustion.

You will find calcium in milk and all milk products, e.g. hard cheese such as cheddar and parmesan; in carrots, kale, Brussels sprouts, watercress and almonds; and tinned fish such as sardines and pilchards (which are about the only tinned food you should consider) where the bones can be eaten as they are so soft.

Carbohydrates These provide energy but can cause sluggishness and excessive weight gain if taken in excess. They are stored as fat if they are not 'burned up' through various activities.

Carbohydrates can be found in foods such as potatoes, pasta and rice (which are also high in fibre), as well as in sweet things such as biscuits, bread, cakes, jams, pastry and sweetened breakfast cereal where the intake must be monitored carefully due to the lack of fibre coupled with the high sugar content. Admittedly these do provide instant energy but as soon as the effect has worn off, you will probably still feel hungry and more tired so, as mentioned previously, try to eat a piece of fruit instead of cakes or buns.

Although honey has a high carbohydrate content, it is a good source of energy. It is absorbed into the bloodstream and released slowly as energy.

Recommended for	*Supplement*
Low blood pressure	Dark chocolate, offal, red meat, mushrooms, green veg., parsley
High blood pressure	Leafy green veg., offal, egg yolk, grains, strawberries
Anti-depressant	Fresh fruit and veg. juices, raspberry leaf tea
Clear skin	Leafy green and yellow veg., egg yolk, fish, offal, water, fresh fruit
Excess weight gain	Avoid all sugar, confectionery, cakes and biscuits
To prevent fluid retention	Raw onion, dandelion leaves, radishes, parsley juice, watch salt intake
Eyes	Leafy green veg., citrus fruit, watercress, bananas, dairy produce, offal, fish
Constipation	Apples, figs, peaches, plums, strawberries, veg. with skins retained, cereals and pulses, fibre
Gums, teeth & bones	Fresh fruit and veg., hard tap water, cereals, pulses

Sex During Pregnancy

As a rule, sex during pregnancy is not at all harmful as your partner's penis cannot harm the growing baby which is well protected in its bag of amniotic fluid and sealed with a mucous plug.

If, however, you have had a history of miscarriages, it is advisable to check with your doctor to put your mind at rest. You may be advised to abstain for the first twelve to fourteen weeks if you have certain medical problems or if you experienced bleeding at the beginning of the pregnancy, just until the baby has had time to establish itself.

Your sexual drive may increase, as psychologically you have no worries regarding contraception, and you may experience a new closeness towards your partner and a certain sense of freedom; if this is the case, make the most of it!

Your sex drive could, on the other hand, decrease, due to the fact that you may be racked by nausea, sickness, tiredness or all three; you may subconsciously worry that you will be harming your unborn child; or perhaps you just want to sleep. Whatever your reason, both you and your partner need to keep in touch with each other physically and emotionally and there are other ways of fulfilling these needs besides intercourse.

Learn to touch, caress or just cuddle to let each other know how much you do still care, and remember, lovemaking doesn't have to be restricted to when you collapse into bed at night, exhausted!

If you're tired of cooking and your partner looks as if a few too many heavy business lunches, or too much stodge in the local 'greasy spoon', have been the order of the day, gather together a healthy picnic. Choose fresh uncooked, crunchy vegetables with, perhaps, a variety of meats or cheeses; rustle up a few simple dips; some good wholemeal bread; and some fresh, easy-to-eat fruit. Now surround yourself with a few pillows and have your picnic in bed – enjoy yourselves!

Although you may find your size an embarrassment and you may not be feeling very attractive, just remember, you are still the same person you always were. Perhaps you will find your breasts are too tender and that any pressure can make them feel very sore. Discuss your worries with your partner and don't feel you have to put on a brave face and have sex if you're not happy about it, or if you are not comfortable.

Try different positions for love making: you can kneel over your

97

man and thus have more control over his penetration (**Fig. 97**), but do go carefully on your knees and try not to 'bounce' around as you could end up having a good sex life but with pulled ligaments around the knees!

Lying on your side with your partner behind can also be satisfying and again you can still control his penetration.

Kneeling over, with your partner behind (**Fig. 98**) can be great fun but, remember, in this position, you have less control and he might get carried away and unintentionally hurt you.

98

By all means lie on your back, but stop *immediately* if you begin to feel dizzy. Because of the obvious bulge, your partner should make every effort to keep his weight off your abdomen.

Whichever position you choose, make sure your back is safe. Now is not the time to practise hanging from chandeliers – figuratively speaking! And remember, while you are making love, you can always practise your pelvic floor exercises (see page 64). They can certainly add spice to your sex life!

Part 3

Postnatal Exercise

Shaping Up Again

Do not attempt to rush into an exercise regime as soon as you have given birth. You must get back into shape gradually. If you have a hospital birth, listen to the advice of the physiotherapist; if you have a home birth, ask your midwife for advice especially if there are complications. If you want to diversify from what you are shown, or from the following exercises, ask their opinion first otherwise you could harm yourself. Remember, your tummy muscles have been stretched to their limit over the past nine months and it will take time for them to revert back to their prenatal state so don't become disheartened or depressed when you still notice a 'bump' – it *will* disappear but only with time and effort!

The very first exercise you should attempt after the birth of your child is for the pelvic floor muscles and this can be done virtually straight away unless you are advised otherwise. The more these can be strengthened, the less likelihood there is of a prolapse of the uterus. The quicker you can get feeling back into this area, the better.

As soon as you are 'tidied up' – stitched etc – try to locate the pelvic floors. You may have to concentrate very hard but if you practise your exercises religiously during pregnancy, you should be able to locate some feeling very soon afterwards. Turn to page 64 to refresh your memory on techniques.

The following exercises are aimed to help you recover your abdominal muscles and to strengthen your back during the first few days and up to six weeks following the birth. Never exercise to the point of exhaustion; just try to get into some sort of gentle routine to help you get back into shape gradually. Don't attempt anything about which you're not sure and never diversify on to demanding workouts until you have had your six week postnatal check-up. It is important that you keep this appointment as any problems can soon be rectified; if you decide not to keep the appointment, you may regret it later on.

If you have to have stitches, you will probably feel very uncomfortable and will dread going to the toilet for fear of stinging, straining and perhaps bursting the stitches (which is, incidentally, practically impossible). To take away the sting, pour cold water on the urethra during and after urination. To relieve a certain amount of the pain after an episiotomy when you feel the need to have a bowel movement, press a thick wad of soft tissues on the stitches while you 'perform'. When you've finished, spray the area with water (you can spend rather a lot on a 'special' sprayer, or you can use a plant sprayer) and either tissue dry or use a hair dryer but make sure you're well out of the bathroom if you do use the dryer.

Breathing correctly will help with your exercises, but trying to co-ordinate breathing with working may be confusing. Therefore, try to think on these lines: when your limbs come towards each other, breathe out, when they move away, breathe in.

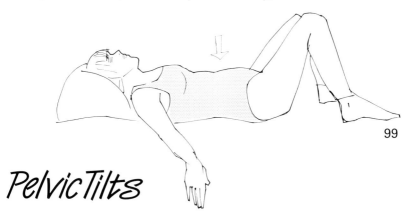

99

PelvicTilts

Wake up your abdominals by lying on your bed with your knees bent and with the feet flat ('crook' lying). Place a pillow beneath your head. Pull in your tummy muscles firmly and elongate the muscles in the small of your back by pushing it down hard against the bed while breathing out (**Fig. 99**). Hold for a count of four. As you release, breathe in. Try four repetitions every hour to begin with. Don't breathe too deeply though, otherwise you may experience dizziness.

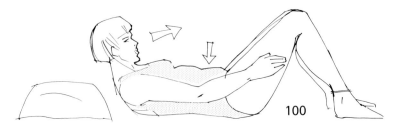

Tummy Toners

1 Still in the same position, again, pull in your abdominals (this is imperative in order to protect your back) and press the small of your back against the bed. This time, hold on to the side of your thighs.

2 Bring your chin on to your chest (giving yourself a double chin) and lift your head off the pillow (**Fig. 100**). Bringing your chin on to your chest will prevent you from straining the muscles in your neck and will also prevent whiplash as you pull up. If you have your arms loose by your sides there is a tendency to jolt up using the neck and shoulders instead of the abdominals. Only come up as far as you comfortably can breathing out.

3 Lower yourself back down slowly vertebra by vertebra, breathing in. The movement should be controlled, never hurried. To begin with, you may not be able to lift yourself up very much; don't worry, with time and practice you will improve.

It might be a good idea to wear socks for the next exercise to protect your heels from rubbing:

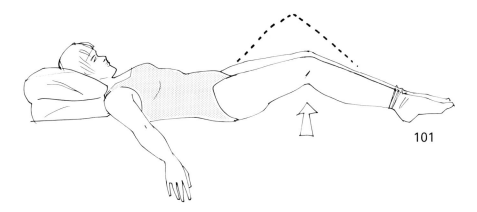

101

1 In the same position but propping your head up slightly more using two pillows (this will encourage you to pull in your abdominal muscles and will help force the small of your back downwards, which protects it).

2 Bend both knees up, keeping the feet flat. Again, pull in your abdominals as hard as you can, down towards your back.

3 Slowly slide your feet away from you breathing out (**Fig. 101**). When you have reached your limit, slide them back up again breathing in. Only go as far as you comfortably can. You will notice progress each day with practice, but it will take time.

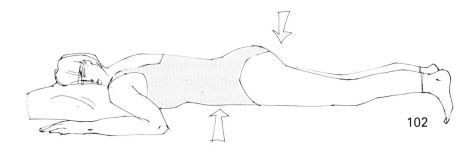

102

Lie on your tummy as much as you can and take advantage of being able to lie flat once again – enjoy it (**Fig. 102**)! In this position, practise pulling in your abdominal muscles and also those in your buttocks. Tense them as hard as you can. Breathe normally.

If the last exercise was comfortable for you, try this exercise to tone up the muscles in the bottom. They do tend to become quite saggy. It is imperative that you keep your head down; if you lift it, there is a tendency to hollow your back thus putting strain on it. Pull in your tummy and tense the muscles in your bottom. When you stop tensing the buttock muscles, you must take a rest otherwise you may lift the leg higher than your safe limit and so put a strain on the small of your back. Keeping the legs straight, slowly raise and lower one leg at a time (**Fig. 103**). Start by repeating four times with each leg and then take a rest.

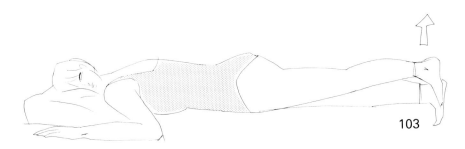

103

If you suffer with back pain after giving birth, do mention this at your six week postnatal check up. It might be a good idea to seek the advice of an osteopath, or masseur, but check with your gynaecologist first. Immediate relief for lower back pain – lie on the floor on your back, and with bent knees rest your feet on the seat of a chair.

Backs

If you do have continual back ache, a good, simple but effective exercise is to sit on a chair with your legs comfortably wide apart and feet flat. Totally relax your shoulders, pull in your tummy muscles, round your back and gently drop yourself forwards as far as you comfortably can (**Fig. 104**). This will slowly stretch the muscles along your spine and across your back. When you feel stretched but relaxed, very slowly return to your sitting position bringing your head up last. Repeat as many times as you can, breathing normally.

104

Part 4
Other Information

Helpful Hints

Brushing the nipples with a soft brush such as a blusher brush will harden them ready for breast feeding.

Massage oil over the breasts, bottom, tummy and thighs to soften the skin and hopefully prevent stretch marks. The action of massage will also help your circulation.

Vitamin E oil rubbed over the perineum will help soften the thick tissue and may prevent you from needing an episiotomy.

Leg cramps: try to increase your fluid intake and practise ankle exercises (see page 50) to improve the circulation. Try walking instead of driving, but don't overdo it.

Wear a good bra, even if you have never done so before, to prevent your breasts from sagging.

Constipation: eat lots of fibre in the form of fresh fruit and vegetables (meat and eggs contain none). Chewing juniper berries also relieves the symptoms. If you have been prescribed iron tablets, check the dosage with your doctor, to see if it can be altered.

Foot cramps: in the fleshiest part of your calf muscle there is a pressure point; if you press your thumb into this as firmly as possible and hold it for a few seconds, this should relieve the pain and relax the muscle.

Nausea: drink freshly crushed root ginger infused with honey. Do not take any over-the-counter remedies without first consulting your doctor.

Varicose veins: wear elastic stockings/tights as soon as veins appear; support hose are not as effective. Put your feet up as often as you can and try not to cross your legs as this will affect your circulation.

Pink/red urine: if you have been eating beetroot, you will probably pass a reddish coloured urine soon afterwards, so don't panic! However, if the colouring persists, consult your GP.

When you attend antenatal exercise classes at the hospital, wear a tracksuit or trousers as you will be taught various exercises which may cause you embarrassment if you are wearing a skirt or your favourite frock.

Insomnia: try taking a warm milky drink just before going to bed. Alternatively, hot orange juice may also help you to sleep. Practise relaxation exercises (see page 68). Instead of counting sheep, count nappies (diapers)!

Diuretic: dandelion leaves added to salads help to relieve fluid retention.

If you are in a low income bracket, and feel you are lacking in vitamins due to your financial state, contact your local DHSS office as you may be entitled to an allowance which will enable you to supplement your vitamin intake.

Weight: try not to gain more than approximately 28 lbs during your entire pregnancy. Don't diet, but at the same time do not 'eat for two'. The more weight you put on before the birth, the harder it is to get rid of afterwards!

To keep the skin of your neck soft and supple while exercising, massage moisturizer in to the neck gently with upward strokes towards the chin. You needn't use an expensive brand; any moisturizer should have the same effect.

If your posture is extremely bad and you are suffering from back pain, ask your partner to massage you. Walk with bare feet at home and practise the relevant exercises to relieve backache (see page 18). If none of these work, try wearing a panty girdle to support the tummy muscles. Do not, however, become too reliant on the girdle, otherwise you may suffer even more after the birth!

Caesarean Elective: this is carried out if there is a rise in blood pressure or if the baby's heartbeat becomes irregular. As it's an 'Elective', you will know in advance that you will have a Caesarean, so watch what you eat to avoid excessive 'wind'; don't go on a binge of baked beans, prunes or too many greens!

Many herbalists recommend pregnant women to drink raspberry leaf tea to help lessen the pain of childbirth. It is debatable how much truth there is in this. However, if you are willing to try, use 2 oz of the dried raspberry leaves and gently simmer them in approximately 2½ pints of water for 15–20 minutes. Make sure you let this cool off completely before straining and using. You might also like to add lemon or honey to flavour. Drink as much as you like but don't keep it for longer than two days.

Home Birth: if you have opted for a home birth, make sure you are prepared well in advance. Make sure there is enough plastic sheeting to protect your bed linen, and that there is sufficient space for you and your helpers to move around in; clear away any obstacles. Ensure that you have clean towels and warm clothes for your new baby. Clear an area for the midwife's equipment. Keep your partner busy; give him/her a job to do in the kitchen to stop you both becoming too anxious. If you need someone, call – they will return in a flash. Lastly, make sure there are bowls or buckets available.

As soon as your waters break, get medical help; if you wait too long, you will be prone to infection. If you happen to be swimming at the time, you may not realize that your waters have in fact broken. However, if you feel a warm sensation around the tops of your thighs, get yourself out of the pool immediately and contact the hospital or midwife.

Wear socks when you go into labour as your feet can become very cold.

You may experience excessive sweating during the final stages of labour; ask your partner to be prepared to sponge you down.

Make sure you keep your mouth moist during labour; you will feel uncomfortable if it becomes dry.

If you normally wear glasses, make sure they are nearby when you go into labour so that you can see what you have produced; it's amazing how many women first see their newborn through a haze as they can't find their specs!

If you have had a Caesarean section, gently rub vitamin E oil or cream over the scar tissue after it has healed to help it fade.

Brushing the nipples with egg whites (if you don't want to buy expensive creams) will ease the soreness of breast feeding.

Questions and Answers

Q. Can I use the sauna while I'm pregnant?

A. It is not advisable as your body temperature increases during pregnancy and there is evidence to show that very high external temperatures can cause a miscarriage during the early weeks. You might feel too uncomfortable anyway, carrying the extra weight and if you overheat, you could pass out. If there is no help at hand you will be in trouble!

Q. What is the *lina nigra*? Will it disappear?

A. This is the dark line which appears during pregnancy running from your naval down to the pubic area. It is more noticeable on dark-haired than on fair-haired women but is completely harmless.

   Yes, the line does usually disappear after the birth since it is due only to temporary hormonal changes.

Q. Can I use a sunbed?

A. This is not advisable as your skin can react badly to tanning during pregnancy; you could be left with dark marks, which may not fade after the birth, around your nipples, upper lip, and lina nigra.

Q. I'm afraid of needles and pain; what can I do to help myself during labour?

A. Needles may not be necessary; if they are, you will be so busy coping with the birth that you probably won't notice them. However, there will be a certain amount of pain. No matter how fit you are or how many exercises you do, you cannot abolish the pain of childbirth except with certain drugs. If these drugs are offered to you, and you feel you need them, don't be a heroine because you have been brainwashed into thinking a natural birth is superior. Some pain thresholds are greater than others, every woman is different. If you need help, take it – why suffer? You must never, ever feel guilty.

   If, however, you are intent on having a natural birth, practise your breathing and 'mind over matter' techniques (see page 76).

Q. I have noticed stretch marks appearing; they look awful. Can I prevent them from getting any worse? Will they disappear?

A. Once you get stretch marks, they usually stay but they do, however, fade. Some women swear by oiling their skin, saying that the marks can thus be kept at bay. Try using vitamin E oil regularly.

Q. I feel pains down the left/right side of my abdomen; does this mean the baby is growing incorrectly?

A. This is probably due to the stretching of your muscles and ligaments but if it persists, mention it to your GP or obstetrician; it doesn't mean that your baby is developing incorrectly.

Q. My back has been aching so much from four months into my pregnancy; is there anything I can do or is this normal?

A. Try the exercises for posture (see pages 15, 16 and 17) and check in a long mirror that you are standing correctly. If you have bad posture, your back will be 'thrown' and your aches will persist. Try placing a hot water bottle or heated pad on the affected area. Do not, however, take too hot a bath as this can cause dizziness.

Q. I am going abroad and am worried about whether the injections can affect my growing baby?

A. Check with your GP as some drugs can cross the placenta and may harm the baby.

Q. I have heard that eating 'blighted' potatoes can cause spina bifida, is this true?

A. There is cause for concern when eating any 'blighted' food and there is a school of thought that blighted potatoes in particular can affect the foetus.

Q. I have put on just over two stone in weight and am only five months pregnant; should I try to diet as I've read that this is the total weight gain allowed for the whole nine months?

A. Now is not the time to start dieting, but do watch what you eat. Eat sensibly and don't dig into the chocolates or biscuits to ward off hunger. Eat fresh fruit instead which will also give you energy.

Q. Now that I'm pregnant, and my waist is gradually disappearing, I'm becoming increasingly depressed. I used to be so slim before, what can I do?

A. Obviously you are going to put on weight, but for the best reason in the world. Try not to lapse into fits of depression. As long as you have a supportive partner and/or friends, they are all you need to bring you out of this temporary mental setback. Convince yourself that you can and will revert back to your former size and try to pursue other interests not linked with pregnancy. If all else fails, talk to your GP who will be able to help and encourage you or possibly suggest counselling.

Q. I am thinking of having my hair permed but have been told not to while I'm pregnant as it could harm the baby. Is this true?

A. This is debatable. Some doctors do not recommend perming as the fumes inhaled might affect the foetus. Also, the hair becomes fairly dry during pregnancy and will become more so if you have a perm. It is probably best, therefore, to wait until after your baby is born.

Q. Can I dye my hair while I'm pregnant?

A. In a word, NO! Chemicals from hair dyes can enter the bloodstream via the hair follicles. Also, because the texture of your hair does change during pregnancy dying it can have an adverse affect.

Q. At work I have to use a VDU screen. Is this safe?

A. Pregnant women should be advised to wear a special apron when working with a VDU because of the possibility of radiation, which can bring on a miscarriage or cause genetic damage to the growing baby. If you are very concerned, ask to be transferred to alternative work.

Q. When I went to the hospital for my first prenatal visit, the nurse asked me my shoe size. My friend said this is because if I wear smaller than a size three shoe I will have to have a Caesarean section. Is this true?

A. Your shoe size is sometimes relative to the size of your pelvic opening. You would have a Caesarean section if the bones of the pelvis are too small for the baby to be born through, but this does depend on the size of the baby as well!

Q. I just can't get into a comfortable position in bed and am having terrible trouble in getting to sleep at night. Can I take sleeping pills or will this affect my baby?

A. It is wise to avoid all drugs during your pregnancy unless they are prescribed by your GP. Try taking a milky drink before you go to bed and lie on your side with your top leg bent over the other one, using pillows to elevate it.

Q. I have started getting small 'skin tags' (similar in appearance to tiny warts) on my neck, is this normal during pregnancy or does it mean I have some sort of diet deficiency?

A. Many women experience skin tags and this is perfectly normal. Others may notice changes in the pigmentation on the face and hands and, again, this is nothing to worry about. It all usually reverts back to normal after the birth.

Q. I want to go on holiday abroad which would mean flying. Is this safe or will the altitude affect the baby? I've heard that airlines are not too happy about having pregnant women on board? Why is this?

A. Flying shouldn't affect the baby at all as long as you travel in a large pressurized plane. Small unpressurized cabins will affect both yours and the baby's supplies of oxygen. The reason why a number of airlines don't like taking very pregnant women on board is because they may go into labour and in the event of complications, staff would not be able to cope. Do be sensible and avoid long flights when the birth is imminent.

Old Wives' Tales

After giving birth for the sixth time a woman was asked why she never married the father of her children and her reply was 'I was told never to marry as I have a bad heart!'. This is actually a true story and it just goes to show that sometimes you really must spell out the facts. The following are old wives' tales; some are based purely on ignorance while others do contain a grain of truth:

FALSE Nose bleeds are an outward sign of an internal injury to the growing baby.

TRUE Pregnant women are prone to nose bleeds due to hormonal changes.

FALSE If you suffer from a lot of nausea and vomiting, you will have a girl.

TRUE It is a good sign if you experience nausea and vomiting since it means that the pregnancy is establishing itself.

FALSE If the baby is born with the caul (inner membrane enveloping the foetus) over its head, it will never drown at sea.

FALSE If the baby is born with the caul over the head it will die of suffocation.

FALSE Your baby will be born covered with a thick layer of black hair if you are scared by a black animal or a spider.

FALSE You will lose a tooth for each pregnancy.

TRUE You must visit the dentist regularly and should not require any more treatment during pregnancy than you would at any other time. Do inform the dentist that you are pregnant though so that adequate precautions are taken. Also, during your pregnancy you are entitled to free dental treatment!

FALSE Your baby will be born with a strawberry birth mark if you eat strawberries during your pregnancy.

FALSE Smoking means you will have a smaller baby and thus an easier birth: smoking will probably result in a smaller baby, but it certainly *does not* mean you will have an easier birth. Smoking is extremely hazardous during pregnancy and should be avoided at all costs.

FALSE While breastfeeding you need not use any form of contraceptive.

FALSE Once a Caesarean, always a Caesarean.

TRUE If the Caesarean was performed because of an unusually shaped pelvis, diabetes or high blood pressure, you will almost certainly have another, but do check with your doctor.

TRUE If your Caesar incision was vertical (top to bottom) as opposed to low transverse (across), you will probably have another Caesarean.

TRUE If the reason for your Caesarean was a 'one off', e.g. breech, placenta praevia (see Glossary), foetal distress, toxaemia or vaginal infection, it is quite possible that you will be able to have a normal vaginal delivery next time; so check first before panicking!

FALSE If you sit too close to the fire during your pregnancy, your child will have a birth mark.

TRUE Sitting too close to the fire while pregnant will probably result in temporarily mottled skin on the legs which looks very unattractive!

FALSE A pregnant woman should 'eat for two'.

TRUE 'Eating for two' can cause strain on the joints and heart. It will also be very difficult to move the excess weight after the baby is born; try to eat a healthy, varied diet.

FALSE If you eat chillies during pregnancy you will have a bad-tempered baby.

FALSE If you stretch your arms above your head you will strangle the baby.

FALSE Heartburn during pregnancy means your baby will be hairy.

FALSE If you 'carry forward' you will produce a girl, if there is slight spread towards the back you will have a boy.

TRUE Women 'carry' in all directions and this will not determine the baby's sex; it is merely an indication of the position in which the baby is lying.

FALSE When you put a ring on a thread and let it rotate over the bump, if it goes clockwise it's a boy and if it goes anti-clockwise, it's a girl.

FALSE If you squat, you will go into premature labour.

FALSE If you drink cold milk during pregnancy your child will have a deep voice; if this were true half the population would be speaking in double-bass!

FALSE A baby cannot feed on small breasts.

TRUE Small breasts are just as plentiful as larger ones and will adapt to the baby's needs.

FALSE You must alternate breasts when feeding to give the baby richer milk.

TRUE Alternating breasts when feeding will help to prevent the nipples from becoming sore; they take time to harden, hence the need to start brushing them with a soft brush well before the birth.

FALSE Breasts should empty at each feed.

TRUE The baby will take all he/she needs in the first three or four minutes. If you 'express' milk, you'll make the supply more plentiful and if you 'express' too much, you could become engorged (crammed full) which can be very painful and extremely uncomfortable.

FALSE Breastfeeding makes you tired. Any number of things may cause tiredness. Recovering from the birth alone will sap a lot of your energy and you will need plenty of rest. Avoid getting tense and stressed as the baby can sense tension and will become restless and upset itself. When you breastfeed, take time to put your feet up and make sure your baby is propped up towards you (resting on a pillow or similar) rather than you bending down which will give you backache. Don't try to do too much too soon after the birth.

FALSE If you douche at conception (presuming you know when you conceive) with lemon, the child will be a girl.

FALSE If you douche at conception with vinegar the child will be a boy. It may sting, however, and you could be mistaken for a fish and chip takeaway!

As you can see, a lot of old wives' tales need to be taken with a pinch of salt. Here are some more examples from different cultures around the world:

Persian – When a small amount of salt is sprinkled on a pregnant woman's hair without her knowledge and she then touches her head, the child will be a boy whereas if she rubs her nose it will be a girl.

Jewish – Pregnant women shouldn't visit a cinema showing horror films or visit zoos in case some harm befalls her baby.

If frightened by an animal or insect, a pregnant woman must not then touch her face or the baby will be born marked.

Icelandic – Pregnant women who step over a cat in the mating season will give birth to a hermaphrodite (a human being combining the characteristics of both sexes).

If a woman eats ptarmigan (of the grouse family) eggs during pregnancy, the child will be freckled.

If she drinks from a cracked cup, the child will have a hare-lip.

Irish – If a woman prays to any particular saint during labour, she should have the saint's name included in the child's name for good luck.

Some old wives' tales can be quite cruel . . .

A child born with teeth is destined to be aggressive.
A child born with its forefinger longer than the others will be a thief.

. . . and some expect quite a lot:–

A child born with an extra toe will be wordly-wise and extremely lucky.
A child born with a double crown will be a champion swimmer.

And finally, a much-asked question is whether it is true that if the baby's heartbeat is under 140 it's a boy and over 140 it's a girl. There is an element of truth in this, but research is still being carried out.

Useful Medical Terms

Abdominal Pains These are common during pregnancy. The muscles are being stretched to their limit and some discomfort is therefore inevitable. However, if the pains become severe, report this to your doctor immediately as there could be complications.

Amniocentesis A test carried out on most pregnant women over the age of thirty-five. A local anaesthetic is administered and a needle inserted just above the pubic bone to draw out a sample of amniotic fluid. This test is carried out to see if the child is suffering from any handicaps e.g. spina bifida or Down's Syndrome. It can also tell the sex of the child.

Anaemia A deficiency of haemoglobin in the blood due to a lack of red blood cells and/or their haemoglobin content. If you are found to be anaemic, your doctor will prescribe iron tablets. You should also keep to a good, varied diet and take iron in its natural form (see section on Diet/Healthy eating).

Black Line – see Lina Nigra

Braxton-Hicks Named after Braxton-Hicks, the doctor who diagnosed them, these are contractions of the uterus. They occur throughout the pregnancy although they are only usually felt towards the end. They shouldn't be too painful but will cause a hard, tight feeling across the tummy. Usually they don't last more than a few seconds at a time but they can be uncomfortable.

Cramps Night cramps are common in the feet and legs. Drink lots of liquid (non-alcoholic) and make sure you are not wearing restrictive socks, stockings or track suits with tight elastic around the ankles. For exercises see page 26.

Cystitis An inflammation of the urinary tract which can be an extremely uncomfortable and painful condition causing a burning sensation when urinating. You may even be tempted not to urinate if the pain is severe. Drink lots of water (a glassful every twenty minutes) or try parsley tea. Avoid strong tea, coffee, all fruit juices and alcohol. Do not buy over-the-counter remedies without first telling the pharmacist you are pregnant. Every time you pass urine, wipe away from the front to the back, never from the back passage forwards as this can irritate and keep the infection active. Wear cotton underwear, and stockings as opposed to tights, and wear skirts rather than trousers. Avoid all scented soaps and bubble baths. Do not use deodorized panty liners or vaginal deodorants – bathe in plain water. If the pain is severe, try pouring very cold water over the urethra while you urinate. This is best poured from a small bottle rather than a beaker – it's less messy! Consult your GP if the problem persists.

Fibroids Small knotted lumps in the muscle tissue; they can be tiny – often no larger than a pea. They can, however, multiply and become very uncomfortable. They are very common during pregnancy but tell your doctor about them nevertheless when you go for your check-up.

Heartburn During pregnancy, the body goes through hormonal changes making the ligaments and muscles quite flexible including the sphincter muscle at the entrance to the stomach. As the uterus enlarges, it presses on the stomach and oesophagus thus causing a slight back flow which can taste bitter and acidic. You will also feel an unpleasant burning sensation. Avoid hot, spicy food and anything fried. Sucking peppermints may provide temporary relief although some do have quite a high sugar content! Drinking cold milk may also help.

Lactation Breastfeeding. As soon as you begin to breastfeed, you help the uterus to contract and you also provide your baby with the nourishment he/she needs for a healthy start in life. Breast milk helps your baby to build up resistance against infections as it is full of the essential antibodies. However, if you are unable to breast feed, don't feel guilty, your baby will thrive just as well on the bottle.

Lanugo This lovely soft downy hair is more obvious on premature babies although it can also be present on quite a number of full term new babies. It disappears soon after birth.

Lina Nigra A dark line running down the centre of the abdomen which usually appears around the third month of pregnancy and disappears after the baby is born. This is nothing to worry about.

Lochia This is the vaginal discharge which appears during the days and weeks after the birth of your baby. It starts off as bright red, turning to a pinkish-brown and gradually becoming almost clear. All the time you have this discharge, and if it becomes heavy, only ever wear unperfumed panty liners or sanitary towels, never tampons. It may clear up quicker if you are breastfeeding as the uterus is encouraged to contract, therefore helping to expel the discharge faster.

Nose Bleeds Quite common during pregnancy. If they do happen, just pinch the bridge of the nose firmly; if they persist, consult your doctor, but a few here and there will do no harm.

Oedema Abnormal infiltration of tissues with fluid, causing swelling of the feet, ankles and sometimes the hands, face and neck, usually during late pregnancy. If this occurs, lie down, and rest your feet. It may help to raise the foot of the bed using a few bricks or books, but do make sure these are secure.

Oxytocin Drip The drip used to induce labour.

Perineum The area of muscle between the anus and vagina. This is where an episiotomy (cut) will be carried out if necessary to help with the birth of the baby.

Piles (Haemorrhoids) Knotted veins in the anus. These can be extremely painful and a good diet should be followed to avoid constipation.

Placenta (Afterbirth) The placenta is attached to the inner wall of the uterus which is checked every time you have a scan. It supplies the baby with oxygen and nourishment and the foetus uses it to expel its waste products. It is delivered after the baby is born, hence the term 'afterbirth'.

Placenta Praevia The placenta lies below the baby in the uterus preventing a straightforward birth. A woman with placenta praevia has to be monitored carefully and needs rest; she may even be hospitalized. Her baby is often delivered by Caesarean section. This unusual condition is not uncommon.

Pill The combined pill is usually quite reliable, if taken regularly without causing sickness or diarrhoea, and is possibly the safest form of contraceptive. This should not, however, be confused with the mini pill which has a much higher failure rate even when taken at the same time each day and without vomiting or diarrhoea. If you are on the mini pill, it is worth considering combining it with another method of contraception.

Pre-Eclampsia/Toxaemia A condition which exists usually in late pregnancy causing swelling of the ankles, hands, face and neck. If you are aware of any swelling, do seek the advice of your GP or gynaecologist who will take your blood pressure and will check your urine for protein. If your tests are positive, you will usually be admitted into hospital for bed rest and careful monitoring.

Primigravida A woman who is pregnant for the first time.

Prolapse of the Uterus The dropping of the uterus into the vagina. You must practise your pelvic floor exercises (see page 64) to help minimize the likelihood of this unpleasant and uncomfortable condition developing.

Prostaglandins Used to induce labour and normally given in the form of pessaries. The cervix will dilate and may encourage the contractions to start (also present in lobster, champagne and semen so if you're overdue, eat, drink and make love!).

Pyelitis An uncomfortable infection spreading from the bladder to the kidneys. Antibiotics are prescribed. Symptoms are shivering, vomiting and generally feeling quite ill.

Rubella (German Measles) If you catch German Measles for the first time while you are pregnant, it can cause severe damage to your unborn child, e.g. deformity, blindness, deafness. If you are planning a pregnancy, it is important that you check with your doctor as to whether you have already had Rubella; if not, you will be inoculated.

Sickle Cell Anaemia Sickle cell anaemia is an hereditary condition and can't, therefore, be caught. It is much more common in dark-skinned people from Africa and the West Indies. The red blood cells are weaker and tend to dissolve, and as a result the blood becomes quite diluted. A pregnant woman with sickle cell anaemia will be monitored carefully and may well be given a blood transfusion during labour. She will be susceptible to blood clots in the legs and possibly have painful joints. It is very important to keep warm throughout your pregnancy if you have this condition as the cold and wet will make you feel worse. Try to drink lots of water to keep the kidneys flushed.

Thalassaemia Another hereditary anaemic complaint. Very similar to Sickle Cell. A good varied diet should be adhered to with a substantial intake of foods containing iron (see Diet/Healthy Eating).

Varicose Veins Dilated veins, the valves of which become incompetent so that the blood flow may be reversed. These may occur in the legs during pregnancy due to the excess weight being carried; it is the pull against gravity that causes a blockage in the venous return flow to the heart. This is why it is so important not to sit with legs crossed, or on a chair that digs into the back of the knees. It is also a good idea to rest with your feet slightly raised. Elastic tights are helpful and you may be able to obtain these on prescription from your GP. Never rub over varicose veins as you may 'push' the blood clot and cause damage elsewhere.

Venereal Disease When you have your blood taken at the 'booking in' appointment, you will be checked for VD. If you suspect that you may have contracted any form of VD during your pregnancy inform your doctor or midwife immediately as this can affect your baby especially during delivery when the baby comes down the birth canal.

Waters Breaking of the waters – this is the bag of amniotic fluid which surrounds and protects your baby in the womb. These may come out in a gush or may trickle. When your delivery date draws closer it might be a good idea to wear a sanitary towel.

Understanding Your Co-operation Card

At the hospital you will be given a co-operation card; keep this with you and present it at each prenatal check-up. Although cards vary, you will see a number of abbreviations, the full meanings of which are shown below:

AFP: Alpha fetoprotein: present in the amniotic fluid and also in the blood of pregnant women. If AFP is highly concentrated when your blood is tested, you may need amniocentesis to check that the foetus is OK.

Alb: Albumin (protein) should not be present in the urine but if it is, it could be a sign of toxaemia (pre-eclampsia). You will also be tested for sugar diabetes.

ABO: Blood group type.

BP: Blood pressure.

Br: Breech – the baby is lying bottom down.

Brim: Inlet of the pelvis.

Ce: Caesarean section.

Ceph: Cephalic: baby is in the ideal position for birth, i.e. head downwards.

CX smear: Cervical smear.

EDC/EDD: Expected date of confinement/Expected date of delivery.

Eng/E: The baby's head is engaged in the pelvis.

Fe: Iron: this has been prescribed.

FH: Foetal heart.

FHH/NH: Foetal heart heard/Not heard.

FMF: Foetal movement felt.

Fundus: Top of the uterus: the doctor will check the height of the fundus to see how far advanced your pregnancy is.

Hb: Haemoglobin (present in red blood cells): this will be checked when blood is taken. If you have a low level of haemoglobin it means you are anaemic and iron tablets may be prescribed.

H/T: Hypertension.

LMP: Last menstrual period.

LOA: Left occipito anterior (this refers to the position of the baby's head – occiput).

Long L: Longitudinal lie: the baby is lying parallel to the spine.

LOP: Left occipito posterior.

MSU: Mid-stream urine sample.

ROA: Right occipito anterior.

ROP: Right occipito posterior.

Relation of PP to brim: Brim = brim of pelvis. PP = presenting part, i.e. the part of the baby which will be born first.

TCA: To come again.

T: Term: possible delivery date.

U/S: Ultra sound.

VDRL: Venereal disease.

Ve: Vaginal examination.

Vx: Vertex: the baby is positioned with its head down.

All notes needed each time (Yes/No)	ST. MARY'S HOSPITAL PRAED STREET LONDON, W2 1NY	Hospital No.
IF FOUND PLEASE RETURN IMMEDIATELY TO HOSPITAL		Obstetrician
		Referred by

(Block capitals please)

SURNAME

FORENAMES

MAIDEN NAME

	Date of birth	Age
	M/S/W/Sep/Div.	Date Married

ADDRESS

Country of birth

Patient

Husband

Date of entry to UK
Age at leaving school
Patient   Partner

Race
Caucasian   Indo/Pak
Mediterr   Oriental
Negroid   Other

Religion

TEL. NO.

Patient's occupation:

Husband's occupation:

BOOKING RESULTS (Date:)

HB	
ABO	
Rhesus	
Antibodies	
Sickle	
Rubella	
VDRL	
Diabetic screen	
MSU	
Cx Smear	

FAMILY DOCTOR

NAME:

ADDRESS:

TEL. NO:

NEXT OF KIN:

NAME:

ADDRESS:

TEL. NO:

Shared care   48 hours   Full stay

EDD from LMP	EDD from early U/S

OBSTETRIC HISTORY

Year or data	Place	Durn of preg (weeks)	Sex (M/F)	Weight (Kg)	Child's name. If not alive state reason	Induction (yes/no) & method	Duration of achve labour (hours)	Anal-gesia	Mode of delivery	Complications	
										Mother	Baby
										Mother	Baby
										Mother	Baby
										Mother	Baby
										Mother	Baby

PAST HISTORY.

Heart disease/rheumatic fever	yes/no	Respiratory disease/thromboembolism yes/no	
Specify		Specify	
Urinary infection/renal disease	yes/no	Diabetes/other endocrine disease	yes/no
Specify		Specify	
Psychiatric illness	yes/no	Infertility investigations etc.	yes/no
Specify		Specify	
Operations	yes/no	Allergies/drug sensitivities	yes/no
Specify		Specify	
Drugs	yes/no	Smoking at booking	yes/no
Steroids:		No. per day: Pre-preg: Now:	
Others:			
Blood transfusion	yes/no	Other	
Specify			
Reactions: yes/no			

FAMILY HISTORY

Diabetes	Hypertension	T.B.
Twins	Malformations	

SOCIAL FACTORS

Pregnancy: planned/unplanned

Reaction: pleased/unsure/negative

Social benefit   yes/no

Experience in earlier confinement

good/bad   If bad, specify why

Main social support

Plans for work

Housing

Name of social worker:

LMP			CYCLE			EDD from LMP :		
						EDD from early U/S :		
Normal Yes/No Certain Yes/No ± days			Contraception in year before pregnancy Method: Date stopped:			Date of quickening :		
FIRST EXAM	Height: (cm) Ideal weight: (kg)		Breasts	Heart & Lungs		Abdomen	Pelvic exam	

Breast feeding: Yes/No/Unsure   Pelvic assessment
Antenatal classes: Yes/No
Epidural: Yes/No/Unsure   Date: Signature:

Date	gestation by		Height of fundus	Presentation	Fifths above brim	F.H.	B.P.	Oedema	Urine	
	LMP	early U/S							Protein	Su

HIGH RISK FACTORS

POLICY DECISIONS

Weight	Blood tests	COMMENTS AND TREATMENT	Next visit and Signature

Appendix

About your Amniocentesis

The following information, which you will find extremely helpful, has been written by Professor Beard of St Mary's Hospital, London. He is one of the country's leading gynaecologists and is extremely sympathetic and understanding of women's problems.

ABOUT YOUR AMNIOCENTESIS

What is amniocentesis?

Amniocentesis is an investigation in which some of the fluid that surrounds the fetus is removed so that tests may be performed on it. This amniotic fluid looks clear, but contains cells shed from the baby's skin and mouth, as well as various chemical products of the pregnancy. In the laboratory the cells and chemicals may be used to detect certain fetal abnormalities.

What abnormalities can be detected?

The main reason for performing amniocentesis at this hospital is to detect Down's syndrome (Mongolism). This condition affects about one in every 650 babies born and is due to a chromosome abnormality which is present in all the cells of the affected infant. Although there is a very small risk (under 1 in 1000) in babies of young mothers, the risk of having a baby with Down's syndrome increases significantly once a mother is past the age of 35. This risk at age 37 is about 1 in 250, at age 40 is 1 in 100 and at age 45 is 1 in 40. Other chromosome abnormalities can be detected but they are much less common. They might be found by chance, or an amniocentesis might be requested because a close relative or a previous baby was known to have the condition.

The chromosome test will tell us the sex of the fetus and parents who are keen to know the sex of their baby may be informed of this if they wish. Occasionally we need to know the fetus's sex in order to find out if there is a risk of it having certain sex-linked disorders.

We also test the fluid for a chemical, alpha-fetoprotein, which is present in increased quantity when a fetus has spina bifida and one or two other types of congenital abnormality. Sometimes we may look for other chemicals in the fluid or in the cells in order to detect certain rare abnormalities that run in some families.

We try to perform amniocentesis at around the 16th week of pregnancy (about four months from the first day of the last menstrual period). If there is any uncertainty about the duration of your pregnancy, your obstetrician will already have arranged for an ultrasound scan to find out just how far the pregnancy has progressed. Amniocentesis is not performed before 16 weeks as the quantity of fluid available is too small and because the cells in it do not grow very well.

How is it performed?

Amniocentesis is performed in the Ultrasound Department by an experienced obstetrician. A scan is first done to determine the age of the fetus, to rule out a few abnormalities and to locate the best area of fluid in the uterus. The developing placenta (afterbirth) can also be seen and the doctor will try to avoid disturbing it during the amniocentesis.

When the scan has been done, the skin is cleaned with antiseptic, some local anaesthetic is injected to numb the area and a fine needle is then put through the abdominal wall and into the fluid in the uterus. About 20 ml (5 teaspoonsful) of fluid is removed using a syringe. After withdrawal of the needle, the skin is sprayed with plastic dressing. The whole procedure takes around 20 minutes, but removing the fluid takes only a minute or so.

Afterwards
You will be able to leave the hospital immediately after your test. We ask you to take things easy for the rest of the day, but there are no special precautions you need take. You will read below that problems occasionally arise after amniocentesis and you should look out for abdominal pain, any loss of blood or fluid from your vagina, or a fever. If any of these occur in the few days after the test or if you are worried in any other way, contact the Antenatal Clinic during the day on weekdays, or the Labour Ward at night and at weekends.

Are there any risks in amniocentesis?
The risk of any problems arising from the amniocentesis is very small indeed. Our main concern is that the test might cause a miscarriage. With ultrasound control we believe that the risk is under 1 in 100, although this is additional to the small risk of a miscarriage occurring at this stage of the pregnancy anyway. There is virtually no risk of the needle causing damage to the baby. If your blood group is rhesus negative we will arrange for you to have a special injection after the amniocentesis.

When are the results available?
The chromosome test on the cells takes between 3 and 5 weeks to perform – generally the result is available in 4 weeks. The alpha-fetoprotein result is available sooner. You will usually be asked to make an appointment to see your obstetrician in the clinic for the results about 4 weeks after the test. However, if an abnormality is found we will try to contact you as soon as the result comes through. In about one in twenty-five cases, the test fails for technical reasons (the cells fail to grow, for example) and we shall then contact you and offer a repeat test. So do not fear the worst if you receive a call from the hospital before your clinic appointment – it may just be a request to attend for a further amniocentesis.

What happens if the result is NORMAL?
Your pregnancy will continue as if you had not had the amniocentesis and no special precautions need be taken. You may wish to ask your obstetrician whether your baby will be a boy or a girl – or you may prefer not to know until the baby is born!

What happens if the result is abnormal?
Remember that the odds are heavily *against* this being the case, but if the result should be abnormal your obstetrician will tell you what abnormality has been found and about the effects that this would have on your baby's life and health, as well as the effects on you and your family of bringing up a child with this abnormality. You will then have to decide whether or not to go through and have a termination of pregnancy.

Termination of pregnancy at a late stage (around 20 weeks) is a more complicated procedure than in the early weeks and is obviously emotionally more upsetting. Such concerns need to be set against the problems of serious congenital abnormality, both for the child and for the parents and other members of the family. For some parents this can be a very difficult decision, even though they had thought the matter through earlier; we shall help in any way we can. The method of termination and any risks would be discussed at the time.

Useful Addresses

British Organizations

Active Birth Movement 55, Dartmouth Park Road, London NW5 1SL
Tel: 01-267 3006

Alcoholics Anonymous 11 Redcliffe Gardens, London SW10 9BG
Tel: 01-352 3001

Association for Improvements in the Maternity Service (AIMS)
163 Liverpool Road, London N1 0RF Tel: 01-278 5628

Association for Postnatal Illness 7 Gowan Avenue, London SW6
6RH Tel: 01-731 4867

Association for Spina Bifida and Hydrocephalus 22 Upper Woburn
Place, London WC1H 0EP Tel: 01-388 1382

Association of Breastfeeding Mothers (contact Elizabeth Dudley)
131 Mayon Road, London SE26 4HZ Tel: 01-778 4769

Association of Radical Midwives (contact Ishbel Cargar) 62 Greetby
Hill, Ormskirk, Lancs L37 2DT Tel: 0695-72776

Birthright Childbirth Research Fund 27 Sussex Place, Regent's Park,
London NW1 4SP Tel: 01-262 5337

British Acupuncture Association 34 Alderney Street, London SW1 V4E
Tel: 01-834 1012/6229

British Epilepsy Association 92–94 Tooley Street, London SE1 9SH
Tel: 01-403 4111

British Homoeopathic Association 27a Devonshire Street, London
W1N 1RJ Tel: 01-935 2163

British Hypnotherapy Association 67 Upper Berkeley Street, London
W1 Tel: 01-723 4443

British Institute for Brain Injured Children Knowle Hall, Bridgwater,
Somerset, TA7 8PT Tel: 02778 684060

British Pregnancy Advisory Service 1st Floor, Guildhall Buildings,
Navigation Street, Birmingham B2 4BT Tel: 021-643 1461

Brook Advisory Centre 233 Tottenham Court Road, London W1P 9AE
Tel: 01-580 2991

Cleft Lip and Palate Association c/o National Secretary, Hospital for Sick
Children, Great Ormond Street, London WC1N 3JH Tel: 01-405 9200

Compassionate Friends 6, Denmark Street, Bristol BS1 5DQ
Tel: 0272 292778

Contact a Family with a Handicapped Child Victoria Chambers, 16 Strutton Ground, Victoria, London SW1P 2HP
Tel: 01-222 2695

Cystic Fibrosis Research Trust Alexandra House, 5 Blyth Road, Bromley, Kent BR1 3RS Tel: 01-464 7211

Downs Syndrome Association 12–13 Clapham Common, South Side, London SW4 7AA Tel: 01-720 0008

Expectant Mothers Clinic (British School of Osteopathy) 1–4 Suffolk Street, London SW1 4HD Tel: 01-930 9254

Family Planning Association (see also Brook Advisory Centre) 27 Mortimer Street, London W1N 7RJ Tel: 01-636 7866

Family Welfare Association 501–505 Kingsland Road, Dalston, London E8 4AU Tel: 01-254 6251

Foresight, The Association for Pre-Conceptual Care The Old Vicarage, Church Lane, Witley, Godalming, Surrey GU8 5PM
Tel: 042879 4500

Foundation for the Study of Infant Deaths 15 Belgrave Square, London SW1X 8PS Tel: 01-235 1721

Gingerbread 35 Wellington Street, London WC2E 7BN
Tel: 01-240 0953

The Haemophilia Society 16 Trinity Street, London SE1 1DE
Tel: 01-407 1010

Health Education Authority 78 New Oxford Street, London WC1A 1AH Tel: 01-631 0930

The Herpes Association 41 North Road, London N7 Tel: 01-609 9061

Hyperactive Children 71 Whyke Lane, Chichester, Sussex PO19 2LD
Tel: 0903-725 182

In Touch Trust 10 Norman Road, Sale, Cheshire M33 3DF
Tel: 061-962 4441

Institute for Complementary Medicine 21 Portland Place, London W1N 3AF Tel: 01-636 9543

La Leche League (Great Britain) BM Box 3424, London WC1N 3XX
Tel: 01-404 5011

London Marriage Guidance Council 76 New Cavendish Street, Harley Street, London W1M 7LB Tel: 01-580 1087

Marie Stopes House Family Planning Clinic 108 Whitfield Street, London W1P 6BE Tel: 01-388 0662

The Maternity Alliance 15 Britannia Street, London WC1X 9JP
Tel: 01-837 1265

Meet a Mum Association (MAMA) (contact Kate Goodyear)
3 Woodside Avenue, South Norwood, London SE25 5DW
Tel: 01-654 3137

MENCAP National Centre 123 Golden Lane, London EC1Y 0RT
Tel: 01-253 9433

The Miscarriage Association Dolphin Cottage, 4 Ashfield Terrace,
Thorpe, Wakefield, West Yorkshire Tel: 09532 828946

Multiple Sclerosis Society of Great Britain and Northern Ireland
25 Effie Road, London SW6 1EE Tel: 01-736 6267

National Association for Mental Health (MIND) 22 Harley Street,
London W1N 2EJ Tel: 01-637 0741

National Association for the Welfare of Children in Hospital Argyle
House, 29–31 Euston Road, London NW1 2SD Tel: 01-833 2041

National Association for the Childless Birmingham Settlement,
318 Summer Lane, Newdown, Birmingham B19 3RL Tel:
021-359 4887

National Autistic Society 276 Willesden Lane, London NW2 5RB
Tel: 01-451 3844

National Childbirth Trust 9 Queensborough Terrace, London W2 3TB
Tel: 01-221 3833

National Council for One Parent Families 255 Kentish Town Road,
London NW5 2LX Tel: 01-267 1361

National Deaf Blind Rubella Association (SENSE) 311 Gray's Inn
Road, London WC1X 8PT Tel: 01-278 1005/1009

National Deaf Children's Society 45 Hereford Road, London W2 5AH
Tel: 01-229 9272

National Eczema Society Tavistock House East, Tavistock Square,
London WC1 9SR Tel: 01-388 4097

National Rubella Council 105 Gower Street, London WC1E 6AH
Tel: 01-631 5344

Organization for Parents Under Stress (OPUS) 106 Godstone Road,
Whytelease, Surrey CR3 0EB Tel: 01-645 0469

Parents Anonymous 6 Manor Gardens, London N7 6LA
Tel: 01-263 8918/5672

Patients Association 18 Charing Cross Road, London WC2H 0HR
Tel: 01-240 0671

Pregnancy Advisory Service 11–13 Charlotte Street, London W1P
1HD Tel: 01-637 8962

Release 1 Elgin Avenue, London W9 3PR Tel: 01-289 1123

Scottish Council for Single Parents 13 Gayfield Square, Edinburgh EH1 3NX Tel: 031-556 3899

Self-Help Groups for Parents Under Stress 29 Newmarket Way, Hornchurch, Essex Tel: 04024 51538

Sickle Cell Society Sickle Cell Centre, Willesden General Hospital, Harlesden Road, London NW10 Tel: 01-451 3293

Spastics Society 12 Park Crescent, London W1N 4EQ Tel: 01-636 5020

Stillbirth and Neonatal Deaths Association 28 Portland Place, London W1N 4DE Tel: 01-436 5881

Thalassaemia Society 107 Nightingale Lane, London N8 7QY Tel: 01-348 0437

Turning Point Cap House, Fourth Floor, 9–12 Long Lane, London EC1A 9HA Tel: 01-606 3947

Twins and Multiple Birth Association (contact Jenny Smith), 41 Fortuna Way, Aylesby Park, Grimsby, South Humberside Tel: 0472-883182

Women's Health Information Centre 52 Featherstone Street, London EC1Y 8RT Tel: 01-251 6580

Working Mothers Association 7 Spencer Walk, London SW15 1PL Tel: 01-788 2565

American Organizations

American Academy of Husband Coached Childbirth Box 5224, Sherman Oaks, CA 91413

American College of Nurse Midwives 1012 14th Street, NW Suite 801, Washington DC 20005

The American Fertility Society 1801 9th Avenue South, #101 Birmingham, Alabama 35205

American Public Health Association Maternal Child Health Section, 1015 18th Street NW, Washington DC 20036

American Society for Psychoprophylaxis in Obstetrics (ASPO) (official name for Lamaza) 1523 L Street NW, Washington DC 20005

Association for Childbirth at Home International Box 1219, Cerritos, California 90701

Downs Syndrome Congress 16470 Ronnies Drive, Mishawaha, Indiana 4655544

Holistic Childbirth Institute 1627 10th Avenue, San Francisco, California 94122

International Childbirth Education Association (ICEA) PO Box 20852, Milwaukee, Wisconsin 53220

International Council for Infant Survival 1515 Reisterstown Road, #300, Baltimore, Maryland 21208

La Leche League International 9616 Minneapolis Avenue, Franklin Park, Illinois 60131

National Association for Parents and Professionals for Safe Alternatives in Childbirth (NAPSAC) Box 1307, Chapel Hill, North Carolina 27514

National Sudden Infant Death Syndrome Foundation 310 South Michigan Avenue, Chicago, Illinois 60604

National Women's Health Network 1302 18th Street, NW Suite 203, Washington DC 20036

National Midwives Association PO Box 163, Princeton, New Jersey 08540

Society for the Protection of the Unborn Through Nutrition (SPUN) 17 North Wabash Avenue, #603 Chicago, Illinois 60602

Further Reading

Janet and Arthur Balaskas *New Life* (Sidgwick & Jackson, 1983)

Sarah Brown *Vegetarian Cookbook* (Dorling Kindersley, 1984)

Dr David Harvey *A New Life* (Marshall Cavendish, 1979)

Sheila Kitzinger *Pregnancy and Childbirth* (Penguin, 1986)

Lennart Nilsson *A Child is Born* (Faber & Faber, 1977)

Peter Saunders *Birthwise* (Sidgwick & Jackson, 1985)

Dr Miriam Stoppard *Pregnancy and Birth Handbook* (Dorling Kindersley, 1986)

Heather Welford *Illustrated Dictionary of Pregnancy and Birth* (Allen & Unwin, 1986)

Index